The Spell of the Hav

and the Philippines

Isabel Anderson

Alpha Editions

This edition published in 2024

ISBN : 9789361472329

Design and Setting By
Alpha Editions
www.alphaedis.com
Email - info@alphaedis.com

Contents

FOREWORD

It is my hope that this book about our islands in the Pacific ocean may be of some interest, if for no other reason than that there is at present so much discussion as to whether or not we should keep the Philippines.

Soon after the close of the Civil War my father, who was a naval officer, was sent on a cruise on the Pacific and stopped for a time both at Honolulu and Manila. During this cruise he took part in the occupation and survey of Midway Island, as it is now called—*our first possession in Pacific waters*. Many years later, when my husband and I started on our first trip to the East, I asked my father if he would give us letters of introduction to his many friends there. He replied, "It is a long time since I visited the islands in the Pacific; if my friends have forgotten me letters would do no good, and if they remember me letters are not necessary." Needless to say, they did remember him and extended to us the most cordial hospitality.

The charm of Hawaii will linger forever in our memory—those happy flower islands where the air is sweet with perfume and gay with the musical strains of the ukulele. We lived there for a time before the Islands were annexed to the United States and, on another visit, we had the privilege of accompanying the Secretary of War, Hon. J. M. Dickinson, so that we had exceptional opportunities of seeing both Hawaii and the Philippines, and of making the acquaintance of leaders among the Americans and the natives.

We found the Philippines especially fascinating on account of the great variety they provide. The old world plazas, the flowering Spanish courtyards, and the pretty women in their distinctive costume of piña are all enchanting. Nowhere else in the Far East are the *mestizos*—those of mixed blood—socially above the natives. The Filipinos are unique in that they are the only Asiatics who are Christians. Among the hills, near civilization, live the savages who indulge in the exciting game of head-hunting. The Moros, the Mohammedans of the southern islands, stand quite by themselves. They are very picturesque and absolutely unlike their neighbours.

Secretary Dickinson and Governor Forbes we can never thank enough for the thousand and one strange sights we saw, as enchanting as the tales which Scheherezade told during those far-off Arabian Nights. I only wish I could describe them in her delightful style! Of all the spells what is more puissant than the spell of the tropics—the singing of dripping water, the rustle of the palm in the breeze. In this land you forget all trouble and dream of love and happiness, while the Southern Cross gleams brightly in the sky.

There it is indeed true that

"The flower of love has leisure for growing,
Music is heard in the evening breeze,
The mountain stream laughs loud in its flowing,
And poesy wakes by the Eastern Seas."

I wish especially to say how grateful I am to those who have helped me in one way or another, with this book: Admiral George Dewey, General Thomas Anderson, Major J. R. M. Taylor, Major William Mitchell, Mr. William R. Castle, Jr., and Mr. C. P. Hatheway. Mr. R. K. Bonine was also very kind in allowing me to reprint some of his photographs of Hawaii. My thanks are also due to Miss Helen Kimball, Miss C. Gilman, Miss K. Crosby, and my husband, and to all the others who have been so good as to encourage me in writing the "Spell of the Hawaiian Islands and the Philippines."

THE HAWAIIAN ISLANDS

CHAPTER I
THE BRIGHT LAND

On our first trip to Hawaii we sailed from San Francisco aboard the *Gaelic* with good, jolly Captain Finch. He was a regular old tar, and we liked him. We little thought that in 1914 he would have the misfortune to be in command of the *Arabic* when it was torpedoed in the Atlantic. He showed great gallantry, standing on the bridge and going down with his ship, but I take pleasure in adding that he was saved.

We had an ideal ocean voyage: calm, blue seas, with a favouring trade wind, a glorious moon, and strange sights of huge turtles, tropic birds, and lunar rainbows. We had, too, an unusual company on board—Captain Gridley, of Manila Bay fame, then on his way to take command of the *Olympia*; Judge Widemann, a German who had lived for many years in Honolulu, and had married a Hawaiian princess; Mr. Irwin, a distinguished American with a Japanese wife—all old friends of my father, who, as a naval officer, made several cruises in the Pacific—Dr. Furness of Philadelphia, a classmate of my husband's at Harvard, who was going out to study the head-hunters of Borneo; and Mr. Castle, grandson of one of the early missionaries to Hawaii. He has since written a charming book on the Islands.

After six days on the smooth Pacific, we caught sight of Oahu, the fairy island on which Honolulu is situated. Diamond Head stretches far out into the blue, like a huge lizard guarding its treasure—a land of fruits and flowers, of sugar-cane and palm. The first view across the bay of the town with its wreath of foliage down by the shore, just as the golden sun was setting over the mountain range, was a picture to be remembered. And in the distance, above Honolulu, the extinct crater called Punchbowl could be seen, out of which the gods of old no doubt drank and made merry.

An ancient Hawaiian myth of the creation tells how Wakea, "the beginning," married Papa, "the earth," and they lived in darkness until Papa produced a gourd calabash. Wakea threw its cover into the air, and it became heaven. The pulp and seeds formed the sky, the sun, moon and stars. The juice was the rain, and out of the bowl the land and sea were created. This country they lived in and called it Hawaii, "the Bright Land." There are many legends told of Papa by the islanders of the Pacific. She traveled far, and had many husbands and children, among whom were "the father of winds and storms," and "the father of forests."

As we approached the dock, we forgot to watch the frolicking porpoises and the silver flying fish, at sight of the daring natives on their boards riding the surf that broke over the coral reef. The only familiar face we saw on the wharf as we landed was Mr. George Carter, a friend of my husband's, who has since been Governor of the Islands.

Oahu is a beautiful island, and the town of Honolulu at once casts its spell upon you, with the luxuriance of its tropical gardens. There is the spreading Poinciana regia, a tree gorgeous with flowers of flame colour, and the "pride of India," with delicate mauve blossoms; there are trees with streaming yellow clusters, called "golden showers," and superb date and cocoanut and royal palms, and various kinds of acacia. Bougainvilleas, passion-flowers, alamanders and bignonias drape verandas and cover walls. There are hedges of hibiscus and night-blooming cereus, and masses of flowering shrubs. Everywhere there is perfume, colour and profusion, the greatest wealth of vegetation, all kept in the most perfect freshness by constant little passing showers—"marvelous rain, that powders one without wetting him!" Honolulu is well named, the word meaning "abundance of peace," for we found the gardens of the town filled with cooing doves. It is said the place was called after a chief by that name in the time of Kakuhihewa, the only great king of Oahu who is mentioned before Kamehameha I.

ROYAL HAWAIIAN HOTEL.

At the time of this visit, in 1897, the total isolation of the Islands was impressive, absolutely cut off, as they were, except for steamers. Sometimes, moreover, Hawaii was three weeks without an arrival, so that the coming of a steamer was a real event. To cable home, one had to send the message by a ship to Japan and so on around the world.

After a night at the old Royal Hawaiian Hotel, big and rambling, in the center of a pretty garden, we started housekeeping for ourselves in a little bungalow on the hotel grounds, with a Chinaman for maid of all work. Here we lived as if in a dream, reveling in the beauty of land and sea, of trees and flowers, enjoying the hospitality for which the Islands are famous, and exploring as far as we could some of the enchanting spots of this heaven on earth.

We were pleased with our little house, with its wide veranda, or *lanai*, as it is called there, which we made comfortable and pretty with long wicker chairs and Chinese lanterns. Mangoes falling with a thump to the ground outside, and lizards and all sorts of harmless creatures crawling or flying about the house, helped to carry out the tropical effect.

In the four visits that we have made on different occasions we have found the climate perfect; the temperature averages about 73 degrees. The trade winds blowing from the northeast across the Pacific are refreshing as well as the tiny showers, which follow you up and down the streets. There is not a poisonous vine or a snake, or any other creature more harmful than the bee; but I must confess that the first night at the old hotel, the apparently black washstand turned white on my approach as the water bugs scuttled away. Nothing really troubled us but the mosquitoes, which, by the way, did not exist there in the early days, so must have been taken in on ships.

The Islands have been well called "the Paradise of the Pacific" and "the playground of the world." The five largest in the group, and the only important ones, are Hawaii, about the size of Connecticut, Maui, Oahu, Kauai and Molokai. The small ones are not worth mentioning, as they have only cattle and sheep and a few herdsmen upon them. They are formed of lava—the product of numberless volcanic eruptions—and the action of the sea and the rain, combined with the warm climate and the moisture brought by the trade winds, has resulted in the most varied and fascinating scenery. Mark Twain, who spent many months there, said of them, "They are the loveliest group of islands that ever anchored in an ocean," and indeed we were of his opinion.

At that time the Islands formed an independent republic, under Sanford B. Dole as President, the son of Rev. Daniel Dole, one of the early missionaries. He was educated at Punahou, meaning new spring, now called Oahu College, and at Williams College in the States. He came to Boston to study law, and was admitted to the bar. But Hawaii called him, as if with a forecast of the need she would have of his services in later days, and he went back to Oahu, where he took high rank among the lawyers in the land of his birth, and became judge of the Supreme Court. After the direct line of Kamehameha sovereigns became extinct, and the easy-going rule of their successors culminated in the high-handed attempt of Queen Liliuokalani to restore the ancient rites and also to turn the island into a Monte Carlo, Judge Dole was the one man who understood both parties and had the confidence of both, and he was the unanimous choice of the best element of the population for president.

HON. SANFORD B. DOLE.

Of course we visited the buildings and localities in Honolulu that were of interest because of their connection with the existing government or their history in the past. The Executive Building—the old palace, built by King Kalakaua and finished in the finest native woods—and the Court House, which was the Government Building in the days of the kings; the big Kawaiahao Church, built of coral blocks in 1842, and the Queen's Hospital, all are in the city, but they have often been described, so I pass them by with only this mention. The first frame house ever erected in the Islands deserves a word, as it was sent out from Boston for the missionaries. It had two stories, and in the early days its tiny rooms were made to shelter four mission families and twenty-two native children, who were their pupils.

Oahu College, too, interested us. It was built on the land given by Chief Boki to Hiram Bingham, one of the earliest missionaries, who donated it to his coworkers as a site for a school for missionary children. The buildings stand in a beautiful park of ninety acres, in which are superb royal palms and the finest algaroba trees in Honolulu. Long ago, in the days of the rush for gold to California, boys were sent there for an education from the Pacific Coast.

The great aquarium at Waikiki, the bathing suburb of Honolulu, I found particularly fascinating. There does not exist in the world an aquarium with fishes more peculiar in form or colouring than those at Waikiki, unless the new one in the Philippines now surpasses it. About five hundred varieties of fish are to be found in the vicinity of the Islands. The fish are of many curious shapes and all the colours of the rainbow. Some have long, swordlike noses, and others have fins on their backs that look like feathers. One called the "bridal veil" has a lovely filmy appendage trailing through the water. The unusual shapes of the bodies, the extraordinary eyes and the fine colouring give many of them a lively and comical appearance. Even the octopus, the many-armed sea creature, seemed wide awake and gazed at the onlookers through his glass window.

An afternoon was spent in the Bishop Museum, which is very fine and well equipped, its collection covering all the Pacific islands. I was chiefly interested in the Hawaiian curios,—the finely woven mats of grass work and the implements of the old days. Here, too, was the famous royal cloak of orange, made of feathers from the *mamo* bird.[1] It was a work of prodigious labour, covering a hundred years. This robe is one of the most gorgeous things I have ever seen and is valued at a million dollars. There were others of lemon yellow and of reds, besides the plumed insignia of office, called *kahili*, which were carried before the king. Our guide through the museum was the curator, Professor Brigham, who had made it the greatest institution of its kind in the world.

This museum is a memorial, created by her husband, to Bernice Pauahi Bishop, great-granddaughter of Kamehameha I and the last descendant of his line. Bernice Pauahi was the daughter of the high chief Paki and the high chieftainess Konia. She was born in 1831, and was adopted in native fashion by Kinau, sister of Kamehameha III, who at that time had no daughters of her own. Her foster sister, Queen Liliuokalani, said of her, "She was one of the most beautiful girls I ever saw."

At nineteen she married an American, Hon. Charles R. Bishop, who was collector of customs in Honolulu at that time. She led a busy life, and used her ability and her wealth to help others. She understood not only her own race but also foreigners, and she used her influence in bringing about a good understanding between them.

In 1883, the year before her death, she bequeathed her fortune to found the Kamehameha School for Hawaiian boys and girls. This school has now a fine group of stone buildings not far from Honolulu.

The Lunalilo Home was founded by the king of that name for aged Hawaiians. When we visited it, we were particularly interested in one old native who was familiar with the use of the old-time musical instruments. This man, named Keanonako, was still alive two years ago. He was taught by his grandfather, who was retained by one of the old chiefs. He played on three primitive instruments—a conch shell, a jew's-harp and a nose flute. The last is made of bamboo, and is open at one end with three perforations; the thumb of the left hand is placed against the left nostril, closing it. The flute is held like a clarinet, and the fingers are used to operate it. Keanonako played the different notes of the birds of the forest, and really gave us a lovely imitation. The musical instruments in use to-day are the guitar, the mandolin, and the *ukulele*. The native Hawaiians are very musical and sing and play well, but the music is now greatly mixed with American and European airs.

It was always entertaining to drive in the park, where we listened to the band and watched the women on horseback. In those days the native women rode astride wonderfully well and looked very dignified and stately, but one does not see this superb horsemanship and the old costumes any more. They did indeed make a fine appearance, with the *paus*, long flowing scarfs of gay colours, which some of them wore floating over their knees and almost reaching the ground, while their horses curvetted and pranced.

One of the amusements was to go down to the dock to see a steamer off and watch the pretty custom of decorating those who went away with *leis*— wreaths of flowers—which were placed around the neck till the travelers looked like moving bouquets and the whole ship at last became a garden. When large steamers sailed the whole town went to the wharf, and the famous Royal Hawaiian Band—which Captain Berger, a German, led for forty years—played native airs for an hour before the time of sailing. It was an animated and pretty sight at the dock, for the natives are so fond of flowers that they, too, wear leis continually as bands around their hats, and they bring and send them as presents and in compliment. Steamers arriving at the port were welcomed in the same charming fashion.

Judge Widemann kindly asked us to dine and view his wonderful hedge of night-blooming cereus. The good old Judge who had married the Princess had three daughters; two of the girls were married to two brothers, who were Americans. All the daughters were attractive, and the youngest, who was the wife of a German, was remarkably pretty. It was strange at first to see brown-skinned people in low-necked white satin dinner gowns, and to find them so cultured and charming.

We dined with Mr. and Mrs. Castle, also with old Mrs. Macfarlane at Waikiki. We enjoyed our evening there immensely. Sam Parker, "the prince of the natives," and Paul Neumann, and Mrs. Wilder, too, all great characters in those days, were very kind to us. Many of them have passed away, but I shall always remember them as we knew them in those happy honeymoon months.

All the mystic spell of those tropical evenings at Waikiki lives in these lines by Rupert Brooke:

"Warm perfumes like a breath from vine and tree
Drift down the darkness. Plangent, hidden from eyes,
Somewhere an eukaleli thrills and cries
And stabs with pain the night's brown savagery.
And dark scents whisper; and dim waves creep to me,

Gleam like a woman's hair, stretch out, and rise;
And new stars burn into the ancient skies,
Over the murmurous soft Hawaiian sea."

I took great pleasure in going to Governor Cleghorn's place. He is a Scotchman who married a sister of the last king, and was at one time governor of this island. Many years ago, my father brought home a photograph of their beautiful daughter, then a girl of fourteen, who died not long after. Mr. Cleghorn's grounds were superb—old avenues of palms and flowering shrubs, and shady walks with Japanese bridges, and pools of water filled with lilies. A fine view of the valley opened out near the house. There were really two connected houses, which were large and built of wood, with verandas. One huge room was filled with portraits of the Hawaiian royal family and some prints of Queen Victoria and Prince Albert. There were knickknacks everywhere, and teak-wood tables and chairs, *poi* bowls made by hand, and primitive stone tools. We were served with lemonade by two Japanese servants in the pretty costume of their land, while tea was served by a picturesque Chinese woman at a table on the veranda.

Besides these informal entertainments, there were various official functions. One was a delightful musicale at President Dole's house, in the midst of his lovely tropical garden; also a dinner at the Consul General's, besides several parties on the naval vessels at the station. Captain Book gave us a dinner and dance on his ship, the *Marian*. We had breakfast one day on the flagship *Philadelphia* with Admiral and Mrs. Beardsley—the Admiral was in command of the station. Captain Cotton of the *Philadelphia* also gave us a boating party by moonlight, followed by a little dance aboard ship.

After lunching with the American Minister, Mr. Sewall, one day, we sat on his lanai at Waikiki and watched the surf-boating, which was most exciting, even from a distance, as the canoes came in at racehorse speed on the crest of the breakers. That day L. and I put our bathing suits on, as we did indeed several times, got into an outrigger canoe with two native boys to handle it, and started for the reef. They skilfully paddled the boat out between the broken waves, waiting for the chance to move on without meeting a foaming crester, and then hurrying to catch a smooth place. At last we got out far enough and turned, watching over our shoulders for a big fellow to come rolling in. Then the boys paddled wildly and allowed the crest, as it broke, to catch and lift the boat and rush it along on top of the roaring foam, right up to the beach. On one of our trips our oarsmen were a little careless and we were upset. But instead of swimming in shore we swam out to sea and pushed the boat until we were well beyond the breakers, where we could right it again and get in—which, for those not used to it, is not a particularly easy thing to accomplish. The people on the shore became frightened about us and sent out another boat to pick us up, for we were quite far out and there were many sharks around.

Surf-Boating

By the way, one hears it questioned even to-day whether sharks really do eat men, notwithstanding two men were bitten lately while bathing as far north as on the New Jersey coast. I will simply say I have seen a black diving boy at Aden with only one leg, as the other was bitten off by a shark, and have myself even worn black stockings when bathing in tropical seas because it is said sharks prefer white legs to black.

An old friend of mine, an admiral in the navy, tells this extraordinary story—that a sailor was lost overboard from his ship, and that inside a shark caught the very same day was found the sailor's head. Here is another story even more remarkable than that, taken from Musick's book on Hawaii:

"Why, sharks are the most tractable creatures in the world when you know how to handle them. It takes a great deal of experience and skill to handle a good-sized shark, one of the man-eating species, but the Kanaka boys know exactly how to master them. I used to have a fish pond over on the other side of Oahu, and at high tide sometimes as many as half a dozen full-grown sharks would come in the pond at a time, and when it was low tide it left them in the pond, which would be so shallow the sharks could not turn over. The native boys used to go to that pond, jump astride the sharks and ride them through the water. It was great amusement to see them riding races around the pond on the backs of the sharks.

"Now, if you don't believe this story, if you will charter the ship I will take the whole party to the very pond in which the sharks are ridden for horses. If I can't show you the pond, I will pay the expense of the ship."

A long drive up into the mountains back of the town one morning, took us to Mt. Tantalus, two thousand or more feet high, from which there are splendid views of the plain below and the sea beyond and mountain ranges on each side. To-day there are many pretty summer villas built on its slopes. While we were looking down on the town and harbour far below us, we saw little puffs of white smoke, and long after could just hear the booming of the guns of the warships, American, English, and Japanese, saluting in honour of the President of this little island republic, who was visiting one of the vessels. Then we climbed higher yet, through woods of *koa* trees, bordered by thickets of the lantana, with its many-coloured flowers, up till we could look down into the dead crater of Punchbowl and over Diamond Head, and far off across the sparkling ocean, while the steeply ravined and ribbed mountains seemed to fall away suddenly beneath our feet.

Punchbowl, where in the early days the natives offered human sacrifices, "is for the most part as red as clay, though a tinge of green in its rain-moistened chinks suggests those bronzes of uncertain antiquity." On this mountain top a myth tells us how a human being was first made—a man to rule over this island. The gods molded him from the clay of the crater, and as they were successful and he came to life, they made from his shadow a woman to keep him company. Indeed, many of the natives still believe in gods and fairies, in shark men, owls, and ghosts, and they will tell you stories of the goddess of the crater even to-day.

When we last visited this island thirteen years later with our Secretary of War, Mr. Dickinson, we saw many changes. We were taken to the Alexander Young Hotel in the center of the town, and to the great hotel at Waikiki. The old hotel, where we stayed years before, had changed hands and was sadly run down. How pretty and green everything was, and how marvelous were the flowers! Many new and rare species had been planted.

The changes have been gradual, but to-day Honolulu is a modern, up-to-date American town, with business blocks of brick. The Makapuu Point Light is one of the largest in the world, and Diamond Head crater has been made into one of the strongest fortifications of modern times. Great men-of-war are to be seen off Honolulu, and Pearl Harbour has been dredged. The army quarters on this island are quite fine. There are good golf links, and on the polo field you see excellent players; the field is also used for aviation. The finely equipped Children's Hospital, the Normal School, and the McKinley High School were interesting institutions that had sprung up since our first visit.

To-day, out of a total population in all the Islands of 209,830, Honolulu has over 50,000. Many new houses and beautiful gardens are to be seen. The island now has, of course, cable and wireless communication with the mainland, electric cars and lights, telephones, the telegraph and numberless motors—in fact, every luxury is to be found. There are a number of clubs, of which the University is especially popular, and the Pacific, or British, Club is the oldest. The graduates of women's colleges have formed a club of their own. Schools and charitable institutions and missionary societies are numerous, and the Y. M. C. A. building is very prominent.

The city now has many churches, which are well attended. The Episcopal cathedral, of stone brought from England, is especially fine. The Catholic cathedral and convent have long been established. It was a Catholic priest who first brought the algaroba tree from Central America sixty years ago and planted it in the city of Honolulu. The descendants of that one tree have reclaimed great sandy wastes and clothed them with fodder for cattle.

Our motor trip to Pearl Harbour took us past Mr. S. M. Damon's charming new place with its delightful Japanese garden. We motored to the Pali, a precipice that drops one thousand feet to the plains which stretch to the sea, where in the old days we had gone so often. Now, a stone tablet on its summit bears the following inscription:

"Erected by the Daughters of Hawaii in 1907 to commemorate the battle of Nuuanu, fought in this valley in 1795, when the invading Kamehameha I drove the forces of Kalanikupule, king of Oahu, to the Pali and hurled them over the precipice, thus establishing the Kamehameha dynasty."

In these days of aeroplanes, I gather this myth of the Bird-man of the Pali from "Legends of old Honolulu," by Westervelt:

Namaka was a noted man of Kauai, but he left that island to find some one whom he would like to call his lord. He excelled in spear-throwing, boxing, leaping and flying. He went first to Oahu, and in Nuuanu Valley he met Pakuanui, a very skilful boxer, and they prepared for a contest at the Pali. Pakuanui could not handle Namaka, who was a "whirlwind around a man," so he became angry and planned to kill him. Namaka was as "slimy as a fish." "The hill of the forehead he struck. The hill of the nose he caught." Like a rainbow bending over the *hau*-trees he was, as he circled around Pakuanui. At a narrow place Pakuanui gave him a kick that knocked him over the precipice, expecting him to be dashed to pieces. "But Namaka flew away from the edge.... The people who were watching said, ... He flew off from the Pali like an Io bird, leaping into the air ... spreading out his arms like wings!"

This panorama is one of the wonders of the world; land and sea, coral reef and mountains, green meadow and shining sand, spread out before one's eyes at the Pali. As the road makes a sharp turn and begins to descend toward the valley, we encounter the full force of the trade winds, for through this pass a gale is always blowing. To quote from Charles W. Stoddard, "If you open your mouth too wide, you can't shut it again without getting under the lee of something—the wind blows so hard."

From the Pali we went on to Pearl Harbour, where the United States Government is constructing a great naval station. This harbour, the finest in the Islands, is a deep lagoon, entered from the ocean by a narrow channel three miles in length. At the inner end it expands and divides into two "lochs," which are from thirty to sixty feet deep and with a shore line of some thirty miles. Algaroba forests cover the shores, and the fertile countryside, in which are rice, sugar and banana plantations, promises abundant supplies for the troops stationed here.

Pearl Harbour has really been in our possession ever since the Reciprocity Treaty with Hawaii was signed in Harrison's administration.[2] As it covers ten square miles, the whole navy of this country could find anchorage there, and be in perfect safety. Not only has the bar that obstructed the entrance to the channel been removed, the long, narrow channel straightened, and a huge drydock constructed in which our largest ships of war could be repaired, but barracks, repair shops, a power house, hospitals, a powder magazine, and all the other buildings needed to make a complete station have been erected at a cost of more than ten millions of dollars. Before the drydock was finished it was partially destroyed by an upheaval. The natives' explanation was that the dock was built over the home of the Shark-god, and that he resented this invasion of his domain.

The island of Oahu will soon be a second Gibraltar, we hope. The channel from the sea is guarded by Fort Kamehameha. Fort Ruger is at the foot of Diamond Head, Fort DeRussy near Waikiki Beach; at Moanalua is Fort Shafter, and at the entrance of Honolulu Harbour, Fort Armstrong. There are more than eleven thousand troops stationed there to-day, consisting of field artillery, cavalry, infantry, engineers, signal corps, telephone and telegraph corps, and it is said there will soon be fifteen thousand or more.[3]

A Hawaiian feast, such as they had in the old days, was given in honour of the Secretary of War, so we were taken to the house of a member of the royal family. I was surprised to see how fine these residences were. This man was only part native, and really one would not have suspected from his appearance that he had any Hawaiian blood at all. His wife was a fat native in a *holoku*—a mother hubbard—who directed the feast, but did not receive.

The bedroom in which we took off our wraps opened out of the big ball room. There was a bright-coloured quilt on the bed, and on the walls were many photographs and cheap prints. Here were also royal feather plumes in vases and more polished poi bowls.

The inclosure where we feasted—or had the *luau* or "bake"—which led out of the ball room, was half open with a cover of canvas and banana leaves. It contained a long table covered with flowers and fruit, bowls and small dishes. There were no forks nor spoons, nor anything but one's fingers to eat with. At the end of the meal a wooden dish was passed for us to wash our fingers. Some of the dishes contained raw fish with a sauce. A cocoanut shell held rock salt, the kind that is given to cattle, and a small bowl was filled with a mixture of sweet potato and cocoanut. That was the best dish of all. The roasted sweet potato was good, too, and pork, sewed up in *ti* leaves and roasted with hot stones, was another delicacy. The drink was made of fruits and was very sweet. And, of course, we had poi.

Making Poi

Poi is described as "one-finger" or "two-finger" poi—thick or thin. Native Hawaiians like it a few days old, when it is sour. Fortunately, as this was only one day old, I was able to put one finger-full of the pasty stuff in my mouth, and, on a dare, I ventured another. Poi is made from the taro root, which is boiled till soft, then pounded and mixed with water. Why I was not ill after this feast I don't know, as I tried mangoes, grapes, watermelon, and pineapple, as well as all the other things. Leis of pink carnations were put about our necks. Hawaiian music with singing went on during the meal, and afterward we danced.

The company was certainly cosmopolitan. One of the people who interested me most was a Hawaiian princess, really very pretty, dressed in the height of fashion. Her father was English. Another interesting person was the daughter of a full-blooded Chinaman, her mother being half Hawaiian. Her husband was an American. She told me with great pride that her boys were both very blond. A wild Texan army man also roused my interest, from the point of view of character study; and I must not forget an Englishwoman, who said, on departure, "Us is going now." We found it all very diverting and the people so kind and hospitable that we enjoyed every minute of our stay.

CHAPTER II
MYTHS AND MELES

Native Hawaiians—big, generous, happy, good-looking folk, athletic and fond of music—are in physical characteristics, in temperament, in language, traditions and customs, so closely related to the Samoans, the Maoris of New Zealand, and the other inhabitants of Polynesia, that it is clear they belong to the same race. Although Hawaii is two thousand miles from any other land, the people are so much like the natives of the South Sea Islands that I do not see how the relationship can be questioned. Distance, too, means little, for we hear that only lately a Japanese junk was caught in a storm and the mast destroyed, yet it was swept along by the Japan current and in an exceedingly short time was washed up on the shore near Vancouver, with most of the sailors still alive. The adventurous boatmen who first landed on the island of Hawaii, however, must not only have crossed two thousand miles of ocean in their canoes but crossed it in the face of opposing trade winds and ocean currents.

The Polynesians of those early days, like the ancient Chaldeans, studied the heavenly bodies, and so, on their long voyages, were able to guide their course by the stars. Their vessels, which were double canoes, like those of the modern Samoans, were from fifty to one hundred feet long and carried a large company of people, with provisions, animals, idols, and everything that was needed for a long voyage or for colonizing a strange island.

The legends of that earliest time tell of Hawaii-loa, who sailed from the west to the Islands, which he named for himself. The coming of Wakea and Papa also belonged to that period. While they are mentioned as the creators of the earth, they are said in another version of the story to have come from Savaii in Samoa. They brought with them the *tabu*, which is common to all Polynesia.

Little is to be learned, however, of the history of Hawaii from the folklore of Pacific Islanders until about the year 1000 A. D. If we may believe their traditions, this was a time of great restlessness throughout all Polynesia, when Hawaii was again visited and held communication with other islands, peopled by the same race. It is interesting to remember that this was the century when the Norsemen were striking out across the Atlantic, showing that there were daring navigators on both sides of the globe.

Paao, one of the heroes from Samoa, who settled in Hawaii, became high priest. He introduced the worship of new gods and increased the number of tabus. The great temple built by him was the first in the shape of a quadrangle—previously they had been three-sided. Afterward, he went back to Samoa and returned with Pili, whom he made ruler, and from whom the Kamehamehas were descended.

From the Hawaiian *meles*, or songs, we may picture their life. The men were skilful fishermen, using hooks of shell, bone, or tortoise shell, nets of *olona*-fiber or long spears of hard wood. The bait used in shark fishing was human flesh. When it was thrown into the water and the shark was attracted to it, the fishermen sprang overboard and fought the fish with knives of stone and sharp shark's teeth. No doubt it was an extremely exciting sport.

Along the shores of the Islands are the walls of many fish-ponds, some of which, though very old, are still in use and bid fair to last for centuries longer. Usually they were made by building a wall of lava rock across the entrance to a small bay, and the fish were kept in the inclosure. The wall was built loosely enough to allow the water to percolate through it, and sluice gates were added, which could be opened and closed. They were at first owned by kings and chiefs, and were probably built by the forced labour of the people. Tradition has it that the wall of Wekolo Pond at Pearl Harbour was built by natives who formed a line from shore to mountain and passed lava rock from hand to hand until it reached the shores over a mile away, without once touching the ground. Some of the ponds in the interior of the Islands have been turned into rice fields and taro patches, especially on Oahu.

The sports and games of the Hawaiians, of which there were many, were nearly all associated with gambling. Indeed, it was the betting that furnished most of the excitement connected with them. At the end of a day of games, many of the people would have staked and lost everything they owned in the world.

Boxing, surf-riding and hurling the *ulu*—a circular stone disk, three or four inches in diameter—were some of the favourite amusements, as well as tobogganing, which is interesting as a tropical adaptation of something that we consider a Northern sport. The slide was laid out on a steep hillside, that was made slippery with dry *pili* grass. The sled, of two long, narrow strips of wood joined together by wicker work, was on runners from twelve to fourteen feet long, and was more like our sleds than modern toboggans. The native held the sled by the middle with both hands, and ran to get a start. Then, throwing himself face downward, he flew down the hill out upon the plain beyond, sometimes to a distance of half a mile or more.

INTERIOR OF HAWAIIAN GRASS HOUSE.

The old Hawaiians were not bad farmers, indeed, I think we may call them very good farmers, when we consider that they had no metal tools of any description and most of their agricultural work was done with the *o-o*, which was only a stick of hard wood, either pointed at one end or shaped like a rude spade. With such primitive implements they terraced their fields, irrigated the soil, and raised crops of taro, bananas, yams, sweet potatoes, and sugar-cane.

Most of the houses of primitive Hawaiians were small, but the grass houses of the chiefs were sometimes seventy feet long. They were all simply a framework of poles thatched with leaves or the long grass of the Islands. Inside, the few rude belongings—mats, calabashes, gourds, and baskets for fish—were all in strange contrast to the modern luxury which many of their descendants enjoy to-day. The cooking was done entirely by the men, in underground ovens. Stones were heated in these; the food, wrapped in ti leaves, was laid on the stones and covered with a layer of grass and dirt; then water was poured in through a small opening to steam the food.

The mild climate of Hawaii makes very little clothing necessary for warmth, and before the advent of the missionaries the women wore only a short skirt of *tapa* that reached just below the knees, and the men a loin-cloth, the *malo*. Tapa, a sort of papery cloth, is made from the bark of the paper mulberry.

Hawaiians say that in the earliest days their forefathers had only coverings made of long leaves or braided strips of grass, until two of the great gods, Kane and Kanaloa, took pity upon them and taught them to make *kiheis*, or shoulder capes.

Tapa making was an important part of the work of the women. It was sometimes brilliantly coloured with vegetable dyes and a pattern put on with a bamboo stamp. Unlike the patterns which our Indians wove into their baskets and blankets, each one of which had its meaning, these figures on the tapa had no special significance, so far as is known. By lapping strips of bark over each other and beating them together, the tapa could be made of any desired size or thickness.

In the old legends, Hina, the mother of the demi-god Maui, figures as the chief tapa maker. The clouds are her tapas in the sky, on which she places stones to hold them down. When the winds drive the clouds before them, loud peals of thunder are the noise of the rolling stones. When Hina folds up her clouds the gleams of sunlight upon them are seen by men and called the lightning.

The sound of the tapa beating was often heard in the Islands. The story is told, that the women scattered through the different valleys devised a code of signals in the strokes and rests of the mallets by which they sent all sorts of messages to one another—a sort of primitive telegraphy that must have been a great comfort and amusement to lonely women.

In the early days, marriage and family associations fell lightly on their shoulders, and even to-day they are somewhat lax in their morals. The seamen who visited the Islands after their discovery by Captain Cook brought corruption with them, so that the condition of the natives when the first missionary arrived was indescribable. A great lack of family affection perhaps naturally followed from this light esteem of marriage. The adoption and even giving away of children was the commonest thing, even among the high chiefs and kings, and exists more or less to-day.

There were three distinctly marked classes even among the ancient Hawaiians—chiefs, priests, and common people—proving that social distinctions do not entirely depend upon civilization. The chief was believed to be descended from the gods and after death was worshiped as a deity.

The priestly class also included sorcerers and doctors, all called *kahuna*, and were much like the medicine men among the American Indians. As with most primitive peoples—for after all, when compared they have very similar tastes and customs—diseases were supposed to be caused by evil spirits, and the kahuna was credited with the power to expel them or even to install them in a human body. The masses had implicit belief in this power, and "praying to death" was often heard of in the old days.[4]

Ancient Hawaiians wrapped their dead in tapa with fragrant herbs, such as the flowers of sugar-cane, which had the property of embalming them.

They were sometimes buried in their houses or in grottoes dug in the solid rock, but more frequently in natural caves, where the bodies were dried and became like mummies. Sometimes the remains were thrown into the boiling lava of a volcano, as a sacrifice to Pele.

ANCIENT TEMPLE INCLOSURE.

It is said no Hawaiians were ever cannibals, but in the early days man-eaters from the south visited these Islands and cooked their victims in the ovens of the natives. Human bones made into the shape of fish hooks were thought to bring luck, especially those of high chiefs, so, as only part of Captain Cook's body was found and he was considered a god, perhaps his bones were used in this way.

The *heiaus*, or temples, developed from Paao's time into stone platforms inclosed by walls of stone. Within this inclosure were sacred houses for the king and the priests, an altar, the oracle, which was a tall tower of wicker work, in which the priest stood when giving the message of his god to the king, and the inner court—the shrine of the principal idol. One of the most important heiaus, which still exists, although in ruins, is the temple of Wahaula on the island of Hawaii.

There was much that was hard and cruel about this religion. The idols were made hideous that they might strike terror to the worshipers. Human sacrifices were offered at times to the chief gods. The idols of the natives were much like those of the North American Indians, but the Kanakas are not like the Indians in character.

The oppressive tabu was part of the religion, and the penalty for breaking it was death. The word means prohibited, and the system was a set of rules, made by the chiefs and high priests, which forbade certain things. For instance, it was tabu for women to eat with men or enter the men's eating house, or to eat pork, turtles, cocoanuts, bananas and some kinds of fish. There were many tabu periods when "no canoe could be launched, no fire lighted, no tapa beaten or poi pounded, and no sound could be uttered on pain of death, when even the dogs had to be muzzled, and the fowls were shut up in calabashes for twenty-four hours at a time." Besides the religious tabus there were civil ones, which could be imposed at any time at the caprice of king or chiefs, who would often forbid the people to have certain things because they wished to keep them for themselves.

One is apt to think that in those early days the natives of these heavenly islands must have been happy and free-living, without laws and doing as they wished, with plenty of fruit and fish to eat; but it was not so at all, for they were obliged to crawl in the dust before their king; they were killed if they even crossed his shadow.

As a pleasant contrast to all these grim features, the Hawaiians, like the ancient Israelites, had cities of refuge, of which there were two on the island of Hawaii. Here the murderer was safe from the avenger, the tabu-breaker was secure from the penalty of death, and in time of war, old men and women and children could dwell in peace within these walls.

The curious belief in a second soul, or double, and in ghosts, the doctrines of a future state, and the peculiar funeral rites, all of which formed part of the native religion, seem strange to many present-day Christian Hawaiians.

In all Polynesia the four great gods were Kane, "father of men and founder of the world,"[5] Kanaloa, his brother, Ku, the cruel one, and Lono, to whom the New Year games were sacred. These four were also the chief deities of Hawaiians.

A Hula Dancer

With some concession in costume to Western conventions

Besides the great gods there was a host of inferior deities, such as the god of the sea, the god of the fishermen, the shark god, the goddess of the tapa beaters, Laka, the goddess of song and dance, who was very popular, and Pele, the goddess of volcanoes. Still lower in the scale were the demi-gods and magicians of marvelous power, like Maui, for whom the island of Maui is said to be named, who pulled New Zealand out of the sea with his magic fish hook and stole the secret of making fire from the wise mud hens. His greatest achievement was that of lassoing the sun and forcing him to slacken his speed. He was a hero throughout Polynesia, and his hook is said to have been still preserved on the island of Tonga in the eighteenth century.

Like most primitive peoples, the Hawaiians danced in order that their gods might smile upon them and bring them luck, or to appease the dreaded Pele and the other gods of evil. The much-talked of *hula* began in this way as a sacred dance before the altar in a temple inclosure, while the girls, clad in skirts of grass and wreaths of flowers, chanted their songs. There was grace in some of the movements, but on the whole the dances are said to have been "indescribably lascivious." After the missionaries arrived, the hula was modified, and to-day it has almost died out.

Many of the old chants were addressed to Laka, sometimes called the "goddess of the wildwood growths." These meles had neither rime nor meter and were more like chants or recitatives, as the singers used only two or three deep-throated tones. Curiously enough the verses suggest the modern *vers libre*. The chants include love songs, dirges and name songs—composed at the birth of a child to tell the story of his ancestors—besides prayers to the gods and historical traditions. As some of these early songs have real vigour and charm, I give a few examples.

The following is a very old chant of Kane, Creator of the Universe:

"The rows of stars of Kane,
The stars in the firmament,
The stars that have been fastened up,
Fast, fast, on the surface of the heaven of Kane,
And the wandering stars,
The tabued stars of Kane,
The moving stars of Kane;
Innumerable are the stars;
The large stars,
The little stars,
The red stars of Kane. O infinite space!
The great Moon of Kane,
The great Sun of Kane

Moving, floating,
Set moving about in the great space of Kane.
The Great Earth of Kane,
The Earth squeezed dry by Kane,
The Earth that Kane set in motion.
Moving are the stars, moving is the Moon,
Moving is the great Earth of Kane."[6]

I find the meles to Laka especially pretty, such as these, taken from Emerson's "Unwritten Literature of Hawaii":

"O goddess Laka!
O wildwood bouquet, O Laka!
O Laka, queen of the voice!
O Laka, giver of gifts!
O Laka, giver of bounty!
O Laka, giver of all things!"

"This is my wish, my burning desire,
That in the season of slumber,
Thy spirit my soul may inspire,
Altar dweller,
Heaven guest,
Soul awakener,
Bird from covert calling,
Where forest champions stand,
There roamed I too with Laka."

This one from the same collection is interesting in its simplicity and strength:

"O Pele, god Pele!
Burst forth now! burst forth!
Launch a bolt from the sky!
Let thy lightnings fly!...
Fires of the goddess burn.
Now for the dance, the dance,
Bring out the dance made public;
Turn about back, turn about face;
Dance toward the sea, dance toward the land,
Toward the pit that is Pele,
Portentous consumer of rocks in Puna!"

The Hawaiian myths, I find, are not nearly so original or so full of charm as the Japanese and Chinese stories, and the long names are tiresome. They have, moreover, lost their freshness, their individuality and their primitive quality in translation and through American influence. They had been handed down entirely by word of mouth until the missionaries arrived. Many of the myths bear some resemblance to Old Testament stories as well as to the traditions told by the head-hunters of the Philippines. The legends of the volcano seem more distinctly Hawaiian.

There are many legends of Pele as well as chants in her honour, which generally represent her as wreaking her vengeance on mortals who have been so unfortunate as to offend her. I quote one that is told to account for the origin of a stream of unusually black lava, which long, long ago flowed down to the coast on Maui:

"A withered old woman stopped to ask food and hospitality at the house of a dweller on this promontory, noted for his penuriousness. His *kalo* (taro) patches flourished, cocoanuts and bananas shaded his hut, nature was lavish of her wealth all around him. But the withered hag was sent away unfed, and as she turned her back on the man she said, 'I will return to-morrow.'

"This was Pele, goddess of the volcano, and she kept her word, and came back the next day in earthquakes and thunderings, rent the mountain, and blotted out every trace of the man and his dwelling with a flood of fire."

Another story goes that in the form of a maiden the goddess appeared to a young chief at the head of a toboggan slide and asked for a ride on his sled. He refused her, and started down without her. Soon, hearing a roar as of thunder and looking back, he saw a lava torrent chasing him and bearing on its highest wave the maiden, whom he then knew to be the goddess Pele. Down the hill and across the plain his toboggan shot, followed by the flaming river of molten rock. The chief, however, reached the ocean at last and found safety in the waters.

This condensed story of the Shark King is also a typical Hawaiian tale:

The King Shark, while sporting in the water, watched a beautiful maiden diving into a pool, and fell in love with her. As king sharks can evidently take whatever form they please, he turned himself into a handsome man and waited for her on the rocks. Here the maiden came one day to seek shellfish, which she was fond of eating. While she was gathering them a huge wave swept her off her feet, and the handsome shark man saved her life. As a matter of course, she straightway fell in love with him. So it happened that one day they were married; but it was only when her child was born that the shark man confided to her who he really was, and that he must now disappear. As he left, he cautioned her never to give their child any meat, or misfortune would follow.

The child was a fine boy, and was quite like other children except that he bore on his back the mark of the great mouth of the shark. As he grew older he ate with the men instead of the women, as was the custom, and his grandfather, not heeding the warning but wishing to make his grandson strong, so that some day he might become a chief, gave him the forbidden meat. When in company, the boy wore a cape to cover the scar on his back, and he always went swimming alone, but when in the water he remembered his father, and it was then that he would turn into a shark himself. The more meat the boy ate the more he wanted, and in time it was noticed that children began to disappear. They would go in bathing and never return. The people became suspicious, and one day they tore the boy's mantle off him and saw the shark's mouth upon his back. There was great consternation, and at last he was ordered to be burned alive. He had been bound with ropes and was waiting for the end, but while the fire was kindling he called on his father, King Shark, for help, and so it was that he was able to burst the ropes and rush into the water, where he turned into a shark and escaped.

The mother then confessed that she had married the Shark King. The chiefs and the high priests held a council and decided that it would be better to offer sacrifices to appease him rather than to kill the mother. This they did, and for that reason King Shark promised that his son should leave the shores of the island of Hawaii forever. It was true, he did leave this island, but he visited other islands and continued his bad habits, until one day he was really caught just as he was turning from a man into a shark on the beach in shallow water. He was bound and hauled up a canyon, where they built a fire from the bamboo of the sacred grove. But the shark was so large that they had to chop down one tree after another for his funeral pyre, until the sacred grove had almost disappeared. This so angered the god of the forest that he changed the variety of bamboo in this region; it is no longer sharp-edged like other bamboo on the Islands.

CHAPTER III
THE FIVE KAMEHAMEHAS

Hawaiian myths and traditions are confused and unreliable, and we know little real history of the "Bright Land," the "Land of Rainbows," before the coming of Captain Cook, in 1778. We do know, however, that, in those early days, the different tribes continually carried on a savage warfare among themselves. Not until the latter part of the eighteenth century did there arise a native chieftain powerful enough to subdue all the islands under his sway and bring peace among the warring tribes. This chief was Kamehameha I, or Kamehameha the Great, often called the Napoleon of the Pacific. The authentic history of Hawaii really begins with his reign. His portrait in the Executive Building in Honolulu shows him as a stern warrior.

The Japanese, as well as the Spaniards, had long known of the existence of islands in that part of the Pacific Ocean. Tradition tells of some shipwrecked Spanish sailors and some Japanese who settled there at a very early date. These Islands were, however, brought to the notice of the civilized world for the first time by Captain Cook.

The Englishmen were received by the simple natives with awe and wonder, Captain Cook himself was declared by the priests to be an incarnation of Lono, god of the forest and husband of the goddess Laka, and abundant provisions were brought to the ship as an offering to this deity. Had the natives been even decently treated, there would have been no tragic sequel to the story, but Cook's crew were allowed complete and unrestrained license on shore. As it was, there was no serious trouble during their first visit, but when they returned in a few months and again exacted contributions the supplies were given grudgingly. The English vessel sailed away, but was unfortunately obliged to put back for repairs, and it was then that the fight occurred between the foreigners and the natives in which Captain Cook met his death. It was this famous voyager who gave the name of Sandwich Islands to the group, in honour of his patron, Lord Sandwich. They were known by that name for many years, but it was never the official designation, and is now seldom used.

The discovery of the Islands by Englishmen and Americans was fraught with evil consequences to the natives, as they brought with them new diseases, and they also introduced intoxicating liquors, and it soon became the custom for whaling vessels in the Pacific to call there and make them the scene of debauchery and licentiousness. It has been said that at that time sea captains recognized no laws, either of God or man, west of Cape Horn. We must not fail to note, however, that even in those early days there were a few white men who really sought the good of the Hawaiians.

Isaac Davis and John Young were two of these men. When the crew of an American vessel was massacred these two were spared, and they continued to live in the Islands until their death. They were a bright contrast to most seamen who visited Hawaii at that period. They accepted the responsibility imposed by their training in civilization, exerting a great influence for good, and were even advisers and teachers of King Kamehameha I.

Captain George Vancouver, who visited the Islands three times in the last decade of the eighteenth century under commission from the British Government, was another white man whose work there was wholly good. He landed the first sheep and cattle ever seen there, and induced the king to proclaim them tabu for ten years so that they might have time to increase, after which women were to be allowed to eat them as well as men. He introduced some valuable plants, such as the grapevine, the orange and the almond, and brought the people seeds of garden vegetables. He refused them firearms. Under his direction the first sailing vessel was built there and called the *Britannia.* Vancouver so won over the natives by his kind treatment that the chiefs ceded the Islands to Great Britain and raised the British flag in February, 1794. He left them with a promise to come again and bring them teachers of Christianity and the industries of civilization. His death, however, prevented his return, and Great Britain never took formal possession.

Kamehameha I, who, at the time of Cook's arrival, was only a chief on the island of Hawaii, joined in the tribal wars, conquered the other chiefs of that island, and became king. While this conquest was in progress, an eruption of Kilauea destroyed a large part of the opposing army and convinced Kamehameha that Pele was on his side.

The subjugation of Maui and Oahu followed. At the great battle fought in the Nuuanu Valley, the king of Oahu was defeated and driven with his army over the Pali. Kamehameha was twice prevented from invading Kauai, but some years later it was ceded to him by its ruler.

After the conquest of Oahu was completed, in 1795, it was Kamehameha's work to build up a strong central government. According to the feudal system that had existed in the Islands up to that time, all the land was considered to belong to the king, who divided it among the great chiefs, these in turn apportioning their shares among the lesser chiefs, of whom the people held their small plots of ground. All paid tribute to those above them in rank. Kamehameha I, in order to increase his own power and destroy that of the chiefs, distributed their lands to them in widely separated portions rather than in large, continuous tracts, as had been the custom previously.

Kamehameha was elected by the chiefs as king of all the Hawaiian Islands, and founded the dynasty called by his name, under which his people had peace for nearly eighty years. He adroitly used the tabu to strengthen his power, and availing himself of the wise advice of the few benevolent foreigners whom he knew, he sought in every way to further the best interests of his people. He has been called "one of the notable men of the earth."

The bronze statue of Kamehameha I stands in front of the Judiciary Building in Honolulu. The anniversary of the birthday of the great ruler occurs in June, and is celebrated by the natives far and near. His statue is dressed in his royal cape of bird feathers and decorated with leis of flowers by the sons and daughters of Hawaii.

The strength of character of Kamehameha I is shown in many ways, but especially in the stand he took in regard to liquor, which was having a disastrous effect on his people. When he became convinced that alcoholic drinks were injurious, he decided never to taste them again.

Before the close of his life, he made a noble effort to prevent the use of liquor by his people. All the chiefs on the island of Hawaii were summoned to meet in an immense grass house, which he had ordered built at Kailua, the ancient capital, solely for this council. When they were all assembled the King entered in his magnificent cape of mamo bird feathers, and drawing himself up to his full height, uttered this command:

"Return to your homes, and destroy every distillery on the island! Make no more intoxicating liquors!"

At the death of Kamehameha I, in 1819, his son Liholiho succeeded him as Kamehameha II. Unfortunately, he did not carry out his father's wishes. He was like his father in nothing but name, being weak and dissipated, and easily influenced by the unscrupulous foreigners who surrounded him. Many changes took place in his reign, but so strong had the government been made by his father that it survived them all. Fortunately, too, an able woman, one of the wives of the first Kamehameha, was associated with the King as Queen Regent.

Before the end of the year 1819 the Hawaiians had burned their idols and abolished tabu. It was the influence of Europeans that had led to these radical changes. Early in the nineteenth century the trade in sandalwood sprang up, in return for which many manufactured articles were imported, especially rum, firearms and cheap ornaments. This trade brought increased numbers of foreigners to the Islands, and their sneers undermined the faith of the people in their old gods without offering them any other religion as a substitute.

In this connection, we are told that twice Kamehameha I made an effort to learn something about Christianity. When he heard that the people of Tahiti had embraced the new faith, he inquired of a foreigner about it, but the man could tell him nothing. Again, just before his death, he asked an American trader to tell him about the white man's God, but, as a native afterward reported to the missionaries, "He no tell him." This greatest of the Hawaiians prepared the way, but he himself died without hearing of Christ.

The Hawaiians had now swept their house clean, and they were ready for an entirely new set of furnishings. In a land far away beyond the Pacific these were preparing for them, and the short reign of this second Kamehameha was made memorable not only by the changes already mentioned but also by the coming of the missionaries, in 1820.

Obookiah, whose real name was Opukahaia, was a young Hawaiian who shipped as seaman on a whaler about 1817, and was taken to New Haven, where he found people who befriended him and undertook to give him an education. They sent him to the Foreign Mission School which had been established at Cornwall, Connecticut, for young men from heathen lands. Among his mates were four others from his native islands. It had been his purpose to carry the Christian religion to his home, but he was taken seriously ill at the school and on his death-bed he pleaded with his new friends not to forget his country. His appeal led the first missionaries to embark for those far-away shores. Three young Hawaiians from the school went with them as assistants.

When the Christian teachers arrived, it is said that the captain of the ship sent an officer ashore with the Hawaiian boys. After awhile they returned, shouting out their wonderful news:

"Liholiho is king. The tabus are abolished. The idols are burnt. There has been war. Now there is peace."

The missionaries received a cordial welcome from some of the natives of high station. The former high priest met them with the words,

"I knew that the wooden images of gods carved by our own hands could not supply our wants, but I worshiped them because it was a custom of our fathers.... My thought has always been, there is only one great God, dwelling in the heavens."

The chief Kalaimoku, neatly dressed in foreign clothes, boarded the ship, accompanied by the two queen dowagers, and welcomed each of the newcomers in turn with a warm hand clasp. One of the queens asked the American women to make her a white dress while they were sailing along the coast, to wear on meeting the King. When she went ashore in her new white mother hubbard, a shout greeted her from hundreds of throats! Because the gown was so loose that she could both run and stand in it, the natives called it a holoku, meaning "run-stand." It became the national dress. The queens afterward sent the missionaries sugar-cane, bananas, cocoanuts and other foods, as a token of their pleasure.

The Americans were received kindly by the King after explaining their mission and were allowed to remain in the Islands. They had many trials and privations, but they were strong in their faith, and within twenty years they had the joy of baptizing thousands of converts.

Kamehameha II, fearing the Russians—one trader had actually gone so far as to hoist the Russian flag over some forts that he had built—visited the United States with his queen and then went on to England to ask for protection, which was promised them by George IV. They both died there, in 1824, and their remains were sent home in a British man-of-war, commanded by Lord Byron, cousin of the poet.

When Kamehameha III was made ruler, all the unprincipled white men in Oahu immediately set to work to lead him into every form of dissipation, but they were not to succeed with him as they had with his predecessor. There were men of ability in that band of missionaries, and they had great influence with him. These faithful advisers had a large share in framing the liberal constitution which he granted.

It is of special interest to note that, the year before the constitution was adopted, a Bill of Rights was promulgated, which set forth the fundamental principles of government and is often called the Hawaiian Magna Charta. An eminent writer has given us the provisions of this document.

It asserts the right of every man to "life, limb, liberty, freedom from oppression, the earnings of his hand, and the productions of his mind, not however, to those who act in violation of the laws. It gave natives for the first time the right to hold land in fee simple; before that the King had owned all the land, and no one could buy it. In this document it is also declared that 'protection is hereby secured to the persons of all the people, together with their lands, their building lots and all their property while they conform to the laws of the kingdom,' and that laws must be enacted for the protection of subjects as well as rulers."

A commission was also formed to determine the ownership of the land. By this commission one-third of all the land was confirmed to the King, one-third to the chiefs, and one-third to the common people. As far as possible the people's share was so divided that each person received the piece of ground that he was living on. The King and many of the chiefs turned over one-half of their share to the Government, which soon held nearly one-third of all the landed property in the kingdom.

The first constitution was framed in 1840. About ten years later an improved one was adopted. The legislature was to meet in two houses. The nobles were to be chosen by the King for life, and were not to be more than thirty in number. There were to be not less than twenty-four representatives, who were to be elected by the people. The Supreme Court was to be composed of three members—a chief justice and two associate justices. Four circuit courts were to be established, and besides the judges for these, each district was to have a judge who should settle petty cases.

It was in 1825, early in the reign of Kamehameha III, that Kapiolani, daughter of the high chief Keawe-mauhili, of Hilo, defied the power of Pele. Having become a Christian, she determined to give her people an object lesson on the powerlessness of their gods. With a retinue of eighty persons she journeyed, most of the way on foot, one hundred miles to the crater of Kilauea. When near the crater, she was met by the priestess of Pele, who threatened her with death if she broke the tabus. But Kapiolani ate the sacred *ohelo* berries without first offering some to the goddess, and undaunted, made her way with her followers down five hundred feet to the "Black Ledge." There, on the very margin of the fiery lake of Halemaumau, she addressed her followers in these ringing words:

"Jehovah is my God. He kindled these fires.... I fear not Pele. If I perish by the anger of Pele, then you may fear the power of Pele; but if I trust in Jehovah, and he should save me from the wrath of Pele, then you must fear and serve the Lord Jehovah. All the gods of Hawaii are vain!" Then they sang a hymn of praise to Jehovah, and wended their way back to the crater's rim in safety.

It was during the reign of Kamehameha III that the United States, France and Great Britain recognized the independence of the Hawaiian Islands. Before this news reached the Pacific, however, Lord George Paulet, a British naval officer, took possession and hoisted the British flag, because the King refused to yield to his demands. Five months later, Admiral Thomas, in command of Great Britain's fleet in the East, appeared at Honolulu and restored the country to the natives. In recognition, an attractive public park was named for him. At the thanksgiving service held on that day, the King uttered the words which were afterward adopted as the motto of the nation, the translation of which is: "In righteousness is the life of the land."

The independence of Hawaii was only once again threatened by a foreign power, when a French admiral took possession of the fort and the government buildings at Honolulu for a few days. Indeed, that independence was not only recognized but guaranteed by France, England and the United States.

Many of the missionaries settled in Hawaii, and their descendants have become rich and prominent citizens. Hawaii owes much to them. So far as lay in their power, they taught the people trades and introduced New England ideals of government and education. Two years after they arrived a spelling book was printed, and a few years later the printing office sent out a newspaper in the native language. The first boarding school for boys was started by Lorrin Andrews in 1831, on Maui, and it was not long after that one was established for girls. The Hilo boarding school, which came later, was the one that General Armstrong took many suggestions from for his work for the coloured people, at Hampton Institute in Virginia. Indeed, so eager were the Hawaiians to learn of their new teachers that whole villages came to the mission stations, gray-haired men and women becoming pupils, and the chiefs leading the way.

As early as 1835, Hoapili, governor of Maui, made the rule that all children over four years of age should attend school, and no man or woman who was unable to read and write should hold office or receive a license to marry. Soon after that laws were passed making attendance at school compulsory. Any man who had a child under eight years of age, and did not send him to school, was to suffer various penalties, among them to forfeit the right to cut the kinds of timber that the king set apart for the use of the people. To make this provision emphatic, the following sentence was added: "All those kinds of timber are tabu to those parents who send not their children to school." An anecdote of this transition period is found in a book written by one who styled himself simply *Haole* (a foreigner). In the valley of Halawa, on the island of Molokai, he was entertained at the house of the district judge, a full-blooded Hawaiian. Among the furnishings of the house were a table, a bedstead, some chairs, even a rocking chair. He gives an amusing description of his evening meal in this house.

"First of all, the table was covered with a sheet just taken off the bed. The table service consisted of a knife, fork and spoon, procured from the foot of a long woolen stocking, a single plate, a tumbler, and a calabash of pure water from a neighbouring spring. The eatables were composed of fresh fish, baked in wrappers of the ti leaf, a couple of boiled fowls, a huge dish of sweet potatoes, and another of boiled tara (taro?).... The last thing served upon the table was something which the family had learned to designate by the name of 'tea' in English. This was emptied into large bowls, and was intended for the family group, myself included....

"The cook was a strapping Kanaka, rather more than six feet in height, and would have weighed nearly three hundred pounds. While I was the only occupant of the table, the family had formed a circle on their mats, where they were discussing their supper with the utmost eagerness. *He* devoted his entire attention to me. He was a good specimen of a well poi-fed native. I could see his frame to advantage, for his sole dress consisted of a short woolen shirt and the malo; and his head of hair resembled that of the pictured Medusa. When I first sat down to the table, he took up my plate, and with a mouthful of breath, which was really a small breeze, he blew the dust from it.

"This act occasioned me no small merriment. But when, in supplying me with 'tea,' he took up a bowl and wiped it out with the corner of his flannel shirt, I could refrain no longer. I laughed until my sides fairly ached and the tears streamed down my face.... For a moment the family were taken by surprise, and so was this presiding deity of culinary operations. But on a second outburst from myself, they felt reassured, and joined with me in my laughter. The cook, however, seemed to feel that I had laughed at some one of his blunders; so he dipped the bowl in a calabash of water, washed it out with his greasy fingers, and again wiped it out with that same shirt lap. This was done three times, in answer to the laughter it was impossible for me to restrain. And when he had filled the bowl with tea, and saw that it remained untasted, he put a large quantity of sugar into the huge tea-kettle, shook it up, placed it at my right elbow, and told me to drink *that!*

QUEEN EMMA.

"The evening was closed with solemn devotions. The best bed in the house was placed at my disposal; and upon it was replaced the sheet on which I had just before supped, and on which I slept during that night. The bed was carefully stuffed with a soft downy substance, resembling raw silk, but called by the natives *pulu*, and culled from the tree-fern. The pillows were stuffed with the same material."

Kamehameha III was succeeded by his nephew and adopted son Kamehameha IV. Although he had a violent temper, he had many good qualities. His wife was Queen Emma, granddaughter of John Young, who was very English in her tastes. It was in her honour that the King founded the Queen's Hospital, and it was probably due to her influence that he started the Anglican mission and made an excellent translation of the English prayer book into the Hawaiian language. The harbour of Honolulu was enlarged by him and other improvements were made, and the cultivation of rice was introduced. After his death, which occurred in San Francisco, Queen Emma made an attempt to obtain the crown, but was unsuccessful.

It was about this time, thirty years before my first visit to Hawaii, that my father, Lieutenant Perkins of the U. S. S. *Lackawanna*, was ordered to the Pacific, and for two years was stationed at Honolulu. He spent much of his spare time in traveling over the Islands, even to their remotest corners. He enjoyed visiting the ranches and joining in the exciting though perilous occupation of driving wild cattle down from the mountains, where one's safety depended almost wholly on skilful horsemanship. He ascended to the great crater of Kilauea, went to every interesting locality, studied the natives, attended their feasts and learned their customs. These things were described in his letters, and such a newspaper bit as the following gives a glimpse of the duties of a naval officer.

"The whaling bark, *Daniel Wood*, of New Bedford, was wrecked on the French Frigates Shoal, April 14th. Captain Richard and a portion of the crew arrived at Honolulu after a passage of 450 miles in an open boat. The U. S. S. *Lackawanna* immediately sailed for the scene of the wreck to rescue the remainder of the crew."

Another clipping records this amusing incident: "The Commander of the British war vessel *Chanticleer*, at Honolulu, set his band playing 'Dixie,' alongside the United States steamer *Lackawanna*. The latter retorted with 'Wearing of the Green.'"

While the *Lackawanna* was at Honolulu, an event occurred which was referred to in the discussions of Congress with regard to Hawaiian matters in the session of 1892-1893, as illustrating the policy of our Government. The official record of the Government affords a very complete story of how the United States became the possessor of what is now called Midway Island. It was first known as Brooks Island, but was renamed by our navy department, principally on the unofficial suggestion of the Pacific Mail

Steamship Company, in recognition of its geographical position on the route from Hawaii to Japan.

The attention of Mr. Welles, then Secretary of the Navy, was called to this island as possibly destined to prove of early importance as a coaling station for United States vessels cruising in these waters. Secretary Welles issued an order to Rear Admiral Thatcher, commanding the *Lackawanna* or some other suitable vessel to search for the island and having found it, to take possession in the name of the United States.

My father's letters give an account of this trip. August 4th, 1867, he wrote:

"Just now we are sailing along quietly, although we have been greatly startled and had a few moments of terrible anxiety. One of the men, while furling the top-gallant sail, lost his hold and fell overboard. Of course, falling from such a height, we all thought he was killed. The life buoys were cut away, and the ship hove to, and the boat sent for him, which picked him up and found him but little hurt after all. It was such a narrow escape, we were all greatly relieved when we got him aboard all right. Except this, we are sailing along day after day in perfect monotony, and for two months or more we shall not see a strange face or hear a word of news from home. But the weather is delightful, and my health is good."

"August 24th.

"Breakers have been reported from the masthead, and I hope it is the island we are looking for."

"August 27th.

"Yes, it proved to be the land we were seeking, and now we are lying at anchor off Brooks Island, called after the captain who discovered it a few years ago; and probably never before or since has there been any one there. It is low and sandy, about six miles long, and its inhabitants are only sea gulls and other sea birds, seals and turtles. Never having seen human beings before, they are not in the least afraid of us, and we can catch as many of them as we wish. I have been fishing and caught a boatload of fish and eleven turtles, each one of the latter weighing two hundred pounds and over. We are going to remain here and survey the island, but to-day it has come on to rain, and we are all cooped up on board the ship."

"August 28th.

"Pleasant weather has come again, and I have been out hunting and fishing. Shot seventeen curlew, hauled the seine, caught a boatload of fish and three large turtles; hunted for shells, but could not find any.

"We are going to have quite a ceremony and take possession of the islands for the United States."

Captain William Reynolds, the officer in command of the *Lackawanna*, was very proud of having been concerned in taking possession of the first island beyond our own shores ever added to the dominion of the United States. In his report he well describes the somewhat dramatic and spectacular performance.

"I have the honour to report that on Wednesday, the 28th of August, 1867, in compliance with the orders of the Hon. Secretary of the Navy of May 28th, I took formal possession of Brooks Island and reefs for the United States. Having previously erected a suitable flagstaff I landed on that day, accompanied by all the officers who could be spared from the ship, with six boats armed and equipped, and under a salute of twenty-one guns, and with three cheers, hoisted the national ensign, and called on all hands to witness the act of taking possession in the name of the United States.

"The ceremony of taking possession over, the howitzers and small-arm men and marines were exercised at target-firing. Having hauled the seine and procured an abundant supply of fish, the men cooked their dinner on shore, and the rest of the day was spent pleasantly, picnic fashion upon the island.... I sincerely hope that this will by no means be the last of our insular annexations. I venture to name the only harbour at this island after the present Hon. Secretary of the Navy, and to call its roadstead after the present Hon. Secretary of State (Seward)."

"In 1869," writes C. S. Alden, in his life of Commodore Perkins, "Congress appropriated $50,000 for deepening the entrance of the harbour; the work was begun, but the amount proved insufficient for completing the plan. One hundred miles to the west, Lieutenant-Commander Sicard, of the U. S. S. *Saginaw*, who had the duties of inspecting and assisting in this work, had the misfortune to wreck his ship on a reef. The hazardous voyage of Lieutenant Talbot with three men in a small boat sailing over 1500 miles to Kauai, Hawaiian Islands, to gain succour, and the drowning of all but one of the men just as they reached their destination and were pushing through the surf to make a landing, is one of the thrilling tales of the sea. Nothing further seems to have been done by our Government until three or four decades later, when it sought to insure safety to navigation by establishing there a lighthouse and buoys. After the visits of the *Lackawanna* and the

Saginaw, the islands were deserted until the Pacific Commercial Cable Company placed there a station in the San Francisco-Manila line, maintaining about forty men. This is the intermediate station between Honolulu and Guam."[7]

Kamehameha V was the older brother of the last King, and a man of autocratic temper, who promulgated a new constitution that increased the powers of the king and decreased those of the people. He was called Prince Lot before he came to the throne. During his reign the leper colony on Molokai was started, in an effort to stop the spread of leprosy. As every one knows, it was here that Father Damien, the Catholic priest, devoted his life to caring for the sufferers and finally succumbed to the disease. The King died in 1872, the last of his line. Just before his death, he turned to Mrs. Bishop and asked her to become queen. She refused, thinking she could serve her people better in some other way, and the King passed away without naming his successor.

It was suggested that either the sister of Kamehameha V or one of the high chiefs should be placed on the throne, but Prince Lunalilo, the nearest male relative, was elected in 1874 by the people. He was thus the first Hawaiian monarch to be chosen by popular vote. His reign, however, lasted little more than a year.

KING KALAKAUA AND STAFF.

David Kalakaua, a high chief, was the choice of the people to succeed Lunalilo. The Reciprocity Treaty with the United States was the great commercial event of this reign. By this sugar and some other products were admitted into America free of duty.

This last of all the kings sought continually to regain the authority lost by the crown when the first constitution was granted, and his government kept growing more arbitrary and corrupt. Finally, so much feeling was roused that the foreign element compelled Kalakaua to proclaim a new constitution, by which he lost the power he had previously possessed and white men gained more control of the government. Two years later, the "Wilcox rebellion," headed by Robert W. Wilcox, a half-breed, was the unsuccessful attempt of the natives to assert themselves against the whites. It was, however, promptly put down.

Kalakaua was kind-hearted, popular, and possessed a dignity and ease of manner that made him at home in any society, although he was dissipated and corrupt and could be "hail fellow well met" with carousers. Captain Lucien Young says of him in his book, "Real Hawaii":

"Kalakaua was only a high chief, in no way related to the extinct royal family, and was reputed to be the illegitimate son of a negro cobbler, who had emigrated to the Islands from Boston."

On the other hand, the sister of Kalakaua, Liliuokalani, who followed him, gives the following account of their pedigree:

"My father's name was Kapaakea; my mother was Keohokalole; the latter was one of the fifteen counselors of the King, Kamehameha III. My great-grandfather Keawe-a-Heulu, the founder of the dynasty of the Kamehamehas, and Keona, father of Kamehameha I, were own cousins, and my great-grandaunt was the celebrated Queen Kapiolani, one of the first converts to Christianity."

King Kalakaua was the author of the Hawaiian national hymn, which was set to music by Captain Berger, leader of the Royal Hawaiian Band. It certainly testifies to a firm belief in the "divine right of kings."

"Hawaii's very own,
Look to your sovran Lord,
Your chief that's heaven-born,
Who is your King;

"Men of Hawaii's land,
Look to your native chiefs,
Your sole, surviving lords,
The nation's pride.

"Men of Hawaiian stock,
My nation ever dear,
With loins begirt for work,
Strive with your might.

REFRAIN:

"Protector, heaven-sent,

Kamehameha great,
To vanquish every foe,
With conquering spear."

Kalakaua died in San Francisco and his body was taken home in a United States man-of-war. His funeral was one of barbaric splendour with kahili bearers, superb feather cloaks, and as was the custom, with bearers who had shaved half their faces and heads.

Under the kings the Hawaiians had a coat of arms. It had on the first and fourth quarters of the shields eight red, white and blue stripes, which represented the eight inhabited islands. On the yellow background of the second and third quarters were the tabu sticks—white balls with black staffs. These were a sign of protection, as well as of tabu. In the center of the shield is a triangular flag, the *puela*, lying across two spears. This also was a sign of tabu and protection. The background represents a royal mantle. At the sides are the supporters in feather cloaks and helmets, the one on the right carrying a spear, the one on the left a kahili, or staff used only on state occasions. Above the shield is the crown, ornamented with twelve taro leaves. Below is the national motto.

Notwithstanding she had married an American, John C. Dominis of Massachusetts, Liliuokalani was even more determined than her brother had been to restore the ancient privileges of the monarch. She revived the old Hawaiian customs, and decided to proclaim a new constitution giving to herself increased power. The English Minister and his followers were on the Queen's side, but those who composed the American mission element were distinctly the best citizens, and this element conquered.

A Citizen's Committee of Safety was formed, then a Provisional Government was established, and a delegation sent to Washington to request annexation to the United States. A treaty of annexation was drawn up, but it was not acted upon by the Senate before President Harrison's term of office ended and President Cleveland's began. In the meantime, Mr. Stevens, our Minister to Hawaii, had, at the request of the Provisional Government, put the Islands under the protection of the Government of the United States. Emissaries of the Queen told their story to President Cleveland, who sent a special Commissioner to the Islands to report on conditions there. After receiving his report, which was far from impartial, the President sent an urgent request—really a demand—to the Provisional Government to restore the Queen to power. It was impossible for free-born Americans to accede to such a demand, and they replied through Hon. S. B. Dole that the Government "respectfully and unhesitatingly declines to entertain the proposition of the President of the United States that it should surrender its authority to the ex-Queen." Then, in 1894, despairing of immediate annexation, they formed a republic with Mr. Dole as president.

It was proposed by some of the people that Princess Kaiulani, Mr. Cleghorn's daughter and the Queen's niece, should be proclaimed queen, and a Regency with Mr. Dole at its head established until the Princess came of age. But the American element did not feel that an honest government would be insured by this means. Kaiulani, who was being educated in England, came here and issued an appeal to Americans, but was unable to awaken sympathy. She died soon after.

The new Republic of Hawaii thus began its history under the leadership of the man of whom it is said that he "throughout his life had been identified with all that was least partizan and most upright in the Islands." It is interesting to note that a vast amount of political wire-pulling was guarded against in the constitution then adopted by the provision that the President at the close of his term of six years should be "ineligible to reëlection for the next succeeding term."

The last native uprising, said to have been instigated by the ex-Queen, occurred in 1895, but was quickly put down. Among the few who lost their lives at this time was Charles L. Carter, brother of Governor Carter. Liliuokalani was tried for treason, with nearly two hundred of her followers, but having formally renounced all claim to the Hawaiian monarchy and taken the oath of allegiance to the republic, she was pardoned. None of the rebels were executed, their sentence being commuted in various ways.

At this time, trouble arose over the large immigration from Japan; the Japanese contract labourers showed a bad spirit; a Japanese man-of-war appeared and also a British war vessel; and it was seen that only annexation to the United States could prevent the Islands from falling into the hands of some foreign power. They were formally annexed to the American republic in 1898. The Territory of Hawaii—this is now the official title of the Islands—has the same form of government as the other territories of the United States.[8]

As was indeed fitting, the first governor of Hawaii was Hon. S. B. Dole. The governor and the secretary of the territory are appointed by the President. Of the fifty senators and thirty members of the House of Representatives about one-half are Hawaiians. There are two official delegates to Washington, one of whom is Prince Jonah Kuhio Kalanianaole, usually called Prince Cupid.

A series of able men have succeeded Mr. Dole, who in 1903 was appointed to another office.[9] Hon. George R. Carter was the next governor until his resignation in 1907. Judge Walter F. Frear held the position from that time until 1913, when Governor Pinkham was appointed, who is still at the head of affairs in the territory.

CHAPTER IV
SERVANT AND SOIL

As Americans have always been leaders in the Islands, so they were the first to begin the cultivation of sugar, which is the chief occupation. They commenced by using their own capital, and then gradually interested capitalists from the mainland. The Reciprocity Treaty between the United States and the Islands in 1876 gave a great impetus to the sugar industry. Capital, particularly from this country, was invested in the Islands, until at present crops of more than 600,000 tons are shipped away in a year.

One of the largest sugar plantations in the world is that of the Hawaiian Commercial Sugar Company on the island of Maui. It was Mr. Claus Spreckles who bought crown land of the Hawaiian Princess Ruth and by his influence with King Kalakaua secured irrigation water for this tract at a nominal rental, then formed a stock company to carry on the plantation. The yearly product of these miles of cane fields alone is 60,000 tons.

On Maui, Kauai and Hawaii skilfully engineered tunnels have brought down the water needed for sugar raising. On Oahu artesian wells have reached "the water of magic power."

We enjoyed an excursion to Judge Widemann's plantation of Waianae on Oahu. Here we saw a sugar-cane mill and wide meadows and brakes of the thick growth, and the whole process of the work—the crushing of the cane into molasses, the refining into sugar—and rode on the tiny plantation railway among the waving green stalks, while the blue sea sparkled on one side, and bare, gaily coloured mountains rose above us on the other.

"THE TINY PLANTATION RAILWAY AMONG THE WAVING GREEN STALKS."

Sugar raising in Hawaii probably furnishes the most perfect example of scientific agriculture to be found under the flag of the United States. "Think of always plowing two feet deep," writes a friend, "and not having to wait for rain, but telephoning to the engineer to start the pumps—of knowing at the end of a crop just what elements and the amount of each have been taken from the soil—of searching the world for parasites to destroy the insect enemies of the cane—of collecting and recording the life history of all the insects found in countries bordering the Pacific and all the islands within its borders, so that when some new pest appears, its origin and characteristics will be known—of sending men out to wherever sugar-cane is grown, in order to study and record its diseases, and giving the planter coloured illustrations of symptoms, so that he may know them in advance of their arrival and be able to check the pest—of the skilful manipulation of the soil, so that there is a constant increase in the production."

In harvesting the cane a path is first opened through the jungle, then the men, armed with knives like butchers' cleavers, go in among the dense growth to cut the stalks. After they have "stripped" a field in this way, the cane must be sent to the mill within twenty-four hours, or the juice will ferment.

Here the Japanese women play their part—for, among the Japanese, the women as well as the men work on the plantations. They gather up the stalks, which are not very heavy but are decidedly unwieldy, and if the field is on high land take them to wooden flumes through which water is run from the irrigation ditches. The women toss the great twelve-foot stalks into the rapid stream which carries them down to a loading place for cane-cars. Here the flume branches into five "fingers," at the head of which stands a man who opens one finger after another, until the cars standing under them are filled in turn.

Inside the cars are men who stack the cane as it tumbles in, so that each car carries a maximum load, laid in good order for the next process at the mill. Here, too, is an automatic "giant-hand" on an endless belt, the "fingers" of which, as it revolves, clutch the stalks of cane like jackstraws and pass them up to a wide belt that extracts every drop of juice so completely that the refuse is fit only for fuel for the furnaces. After the various processes of boiling down, evaporating, crystallizing and drying, the raw sugar is shoveled into gunny-sacks, which are filled to weigh exactly one hundred pounds each. Again the women take hold, and sew up the bags. The cost of raising and marketing sugar is from forty-five to seventy-five dollars a ton.

Japanese women who work on the sugar plantations may be seen sometimes knee-deep in muddy-watery soil near the flumes, or again out in the driest, hottest part of a newly plowed field. They have discarded their usual Japanese dress for a mixed costume, consisting of a close-fitting waist of dark, figured, Japanese cotton crêpe, a scant skirt to the knee, khaki gaiters, and their own heavy cotton "bootees." To protect their hair from dust and their necks from the sun, they wear a piece of Japanese toweling, which is tied across the back of the head and hangs down on the shoulders. On top of this is perched a cheap American sailor hat. The effect is certainly startling. Some take their tiny babies in bright-figured swaddling clothes with them, and put up a little shelter tent of cloth and sticks, where the youngsters lie and sleep.

Most of the women who do agricultural work are Japanese. A few years ago, when a ship-load of people came from Madeira, the women told the immigration authorities that they had come to work on the plantations. But, after a very short time, they retired from this sort of labour for the much pleasanter and more remunerative business of making Madeira embroidery. Among the Chinese the women rarely go out of their own homes to work, although Oriental servants prevail all over these Islands. Some of the younger generation of Portuguese girls go out as nursemaids in white families, but the majority of that race make sewing and dressmaking or "clerking" their means of support. It is surprising, indeed, to see how few of the employees in any store are "white"; bookkeepers, clerks, etc., are usually young part-Hawaiians or part-Chinese.

From the beginning, when sugar was ready for export, it was rarely shipped from the Hawaiian Islands in any but American bottoms. The American-Hawaiian Steamship Company—the largest fleet sailing under the Stars and Stripes and numbering twenty-eight vessels—the Oceanic Steamship Company, and the Matson Navigation Company, were all formed largely because of the favourable contracts they were able to make for carrying sugar, and the Pacific Mail Steamship Company, which plied between California and the Far East, stopped at Honolulu because of the profit to be made by carrying freight from the Islands. American shipping on the Pacific, however, has always been at a disadvantage, because foreign ships can be built more cheaply than ours and are usually subsidized.

As if these drawbacks were not enough, during the present Congress the Seaman's Act, somewhat modified now to be sure, has had a disastrous effect on American shipping on the Pacific Ocean. The American boats used to carry crews of well trained Chinamen. Under this act the majority of the crew must be English-speaking sailors and they cannot be procured in sufficient numbers nor can such boats generally be run with sufficient economy to compete with foreign flags. So trans-Pacific trade has been given over almost entirely to the Japanese, who have especially fine passenger ships on that route to-day. As, according to our laws, these boats are not permitted to carry passengers or freight between American ports, the service between the Islands and the United States has been seriously crippled with consequent increase in rates of carriage. A resident in the Islands writes, "When the last Pacific Mail steamer sailed from Honolulu Harbour, all flags were at half mast and Hawaii was in mourning."

Still, the planters are cheerful. For 1916, they look forward to an estimated production of 603,000 tons and a continuance of the present high prices, which will enable them not only to pay good dividends but also to install labour-saving machinery and to make other improvements, by which they will produce sugar more cheaply when the present era of high prices is over. The shipments of raw sugar from Hawaii for the year ending June 30, 1915, sold for more than $51,000,000.

Next in importance to the sugar industry is the production of pineapples. These are raised only on the higher ground. The land is as carefully prepared as a garden, and the soil thoroughly pulverized. The plants are set in furrows, and there are sometimes as many as twelve thousand to the acre. They mature their fruit in about two years. When the pineapple ripens, from the lower part of the stump suckers appear, which bear fruit one year later. These in turn grow suckers that come into bearing the following year. Besides these there are slips, that spring from the upper part of the parent plant. New plants are grown not only from suckers and slips, but also from the crowns of the fruit, and growers consider them all about equally good. The plants almost never produce seeds, and when found, they are used for experimental purposes only.

PINEAPPLE PLANTATION, ISLAND OF OAHU.

There are 24,000 acres of land in the pineapple plantations of the Islands, and most of them are on Oahu. There is never any frost, and as there are no serious insect pests which attack the fruit the crop is a very fine one. Nor is irrigation necessary, so that thousands of acres unavailable for sugar have brought in millions of dollars to those who own or rent these plantations.

The fields are carefully picked over every day or two, and only perfectly ripe fruit is gathered. Hawaiian pineapples are rich in sugar when fully matured, but if picked green, they contain little sugar, and gain none after they are taken from the plant. Extensive experiments have shown that the Smooth Cayenne variety is far superior to all others, and it is now the only one grown in the Islands. In no instance are the fields more than a few miles from the cannery, and the fruit is put in the tins as soon as possible after it is picked. The Hawaiian canneries are equipped with labour-saving machinery. Aside from grading the slices and filling the cans, all the work is done by machines. The employees who handle the fruit wear rubber gloves with gauntlets, and the most modern sanitary methods are observed throughout. Every night everything in the factory is washed, steamed and scrubbed as clean as possible.

When the fruit arrives at the cannery, it passes into a machine which first cuts off both ends, then takes out the core and removes the rind. It is then conveyed to another, which slices the whole pineapple in one operation. From here it passes on a moving belt in front of a line of workers, who select the perfect cylindrical pieces for the first grade.

From the packing table the tins go to the syrup machine, where the fruit is covered with a syrup made of clear water and granulated sugar, thence to the exhaust box and double sealer, where it is heated and the cover sealed on the can. Then the can is conveyed to the cooker, where it is submerged in boiling water from twenty to thirty-five minutes, after which it is left in the cooling room about twelve hours, and then stacked in the warehouse until required for shipment.

The history of this industry is interesting. Only small amounts were canned previous to the year 1901. There has been a steady increase ever since, with a total output in 1914 of over 2,000,000 cases from nine canneries. Nothing like this rapid increase in production and distribution has ever been known before in the canned-fruit trade. California, as every one knows, is the greatest fruit-producing section in the world, and her canned fruits are found in practically every market, yet her average total pack, of every variety except apples, from 1901 to 1910, was only about one-third more than the pack of Hawaiian pineapples alone in 1914. The total value of those shipped to the United States for the year ending June 30, 1915, was nearly $6,000,000.

Besides the other important staples raised by the planters for export, coffee and rice are produced in large quantities—over 3,000,000 pounds of each. The coffee grown in the district of Kona is famous. The Chinese are especially good at market gardening. The Hawaiians also plant taro for poi, which, although now manufactured by machinery, is still their favourite food, and is also eaten by the whites. Doctors pronounce it most digestible and strengthening. Duke Kahanamoku, a native who has always lived on poi, is the champion swimmer of the world. It is true that not only poi but also the climate is favourable to our race as well, for white boys brought up in Hawaii have proved themselves to be strong, all those who have gone into athletics in American colleges having made fine records.

In addition to the products of the large plantations, wool, hides and skins from the ranches are exported to a considerable extent. The Shipman stock ranch, near Hilo, has been carried on for more than forty years. The Parker ranch, however, is the largest, having 18,000 head of cattle—Herefords and Holsteins. The long pods of the algaroba tree furnish a large part of the feed for cattle and horses. This is the carob tree of the New Testament, the pods of which were the husks that the Prodigal Son fed to the swine he tended. In the earlier days, guano from the bird islands was exported, for use as a fertilizer.

While plantation life in the Islands may be monotonous for the resident, it is full of interest for the tourist who really takes time to see it. An effort is made by the planters to furnish recreation for their labourers. At Waialua on Oahu a large hall has been built, where moving-picture shows are given at intervals, political meetings are held, and there are dances for the white colony. The latter have tennis courts near their homes and hold tournaments, to which they invite players from other plantations. As work is over at four o'clock—the hours being from five to eleven in the morning and two to four in the afternoon—the men who work in mill, store or office can play every afternoon.

The Portuguese, Japanese and Hawaiian boys have formed a baseball team, which represents the plantation in a league of such teams. There are match games by this league at different places every Sunday. The Japanese at Waialua have a theater, the occasional performances at which are announced during the day by a man who drives through all parts of the plantation in a hack covered with Japanese signs, beating a drum.

The native Hawaiians in country districts often present "tableaux" for the benefit of their church or some charity fund. A friend of mine told me she had once gone to a representation of "Adam and Eve" which would have seemed either sacrilegious or ridiculous if done by any but these ingenuous, grown-up children. The minister of the church played the part of Satan, in a bright red union suit with a long tail; a large native, in flowing white robes, with a Santa Claus beard and mask, took the part of the Deity and banished Adam and Eve, in brown union suits the colour of their skin, from the

Garden of Eden. Other tableaux gave very vivid portrayals of scenes from ancient days of royalty, with its attendant pomp and ceremony, and old Hawaiian legends. One of these was about Paahana, a young Hawaiian girl, who was afraid of the white settlers, and ran away to the mountains, building herself a shelter of grass among the bushes. Finally she was discovered by the white missionaries, who tried to approach her, but she was wild with fear, and vanished from sight into the forest. This story was told in verse, sung to the tune of "Mauna Kea," a hula dance.

These entertainments are never complete without a dance for young and old, to music sung and played by a quintette of native boys. Besides the ukulele and the taro-patch, which is a large ukulele with five strings instead of four, they use the mandolin, violin, guitar and bass-viol. The Hawaiians, being naturally musical, have a keen sense of time and rhythm. The Filipinos are also fond of dancing, and in the Libby, McNiel and Libby pineapple cannery, where many of this nationality are employed, dances are held to make them more contented with their isolated life.

Among the plantation labourers there is never the abject poverty that is known in the Far East for, in addition to steady wages, houses, water, fuel and doctor's services are all provided for them. Although the climate is semi-tropical sunstroke is unknown. The men who work around the machinery and the boiling sugar wear as few clothes as possible, and the women who sew up the bags of sugar as fast as they are filled, have adopted the cool and comfortable but hideous Hawaiian garb of the holoku. The heat from the great boilers in the mill is sometimes hard for the white men to bear, but I have never heard of a case of heat-prostration. As a large part of the school work must be done on the plantations I insert the following description, given me by one of the teachers of the school at Waialua, Oahu, the largest outside of Honolulu.

"As the pupils are almost entirely foreign, the first grade has three divisions, to accommodate the number who enter it until they are able to speak enough English to be properly graded. Sometimes one finds here children of twelve to fourteen years who have just come to Hawaii. As a rule, they work hard to get out of the 'baby-grade,' and are quickly promoted.

"I was the only white teacher in the school besides the principal. The other teachers were Hawaiian, half-white and Chinese Hawaiian girls who had gone through the Honolulu Normal School. They are good teachers, kind and patient, and can instruct children in the same slow manner in which they themselves learn. There was also a young Hawaiian man, a Normal graduate, who could help in many extra ways, such as map-drawing, chorus-leading, games, etc.

"Fifteen nationalities were represented in the various grades—Hawaiian, Chinese, Japanese, Portuguese, Filipino, Spanish, Korean, Porto Rican, and a few Scotch, English, Canadians, Germans and Americans, as well as Russians and Italians. Besides the pure bloods there were many mixtures, such as American-Hawaiian, Chinese-Hawaiian, Japanese-Portuguese, German-Hawaiian, etc.

"The Japanese and Chinese were the best pupils in every way. The Hawaiians were tractable, but stupid; Portuguese, smart but mischievous. School hours were from nine to twelve, and from half past twelve to two. Most of the children came from long distances, and after the plantation school was dismissed, the Japanese children went to a Japanese school for two hours.

"In the first grade, I taught reading, writing and 'rithmetic; also nature-study, in simple form, story-work, folk songs and dances. These last helped them a great deal in the new vocabulary, as they loved that part of the day's program.

"It was interesting to note the habits of the different nationalities at recess, especially in regard to their luncheon. The Japanese usually were together out in the yard. They each had their little tin pail with top and bottom section, in which they carried fish and cold rice. I never got a very close look at it, to know how the fish was cooked, but I could smell it afar off! They seemed very shy, and would try to hide their lunch as I walked past. The Chinese were even shyer about their lunch, for they never gathered together, as the other nationalities did, but went to some secluded spot and nibbled away at an orange or something else.

"The Portuguese usually brought long rolls of bread, which had been cut open and a red jelly-like substance spread all along the inside. They also had fruit, and especially the mango in its season.

"A little Japanese store nearby kept cakes and pastries, which were very popular when the children had money, but the greatest delicacy sold there seemed to be a rubbery substance, which looked like a piece of resin, but could be shaved in long strips. They called it dry squid, but it did not seem like the dry squid I've tried to masticate at native luaus, and I never did find out just what it was.

"The schools are all supported by the territorial government, which in turn receives the plantation taxes, so the plantations themselves do not directly support the schools, although the children of the labourers comprise nine-tenths of the pupils outside Honolulu.

"There is compulsory attendance until the age of fourteen, and at Waialua a school policeman—a Hawaiian—went all over the plantations on horseback and found out if any of the children were ill or playing truant."

Each nationality is housed more or less by itself in small, one-story houses built in rows, each group called a camp. The white men employed as chemists, bookkeepers and clerks in the general store usually live in a group near the buildings where they are employed. They are German, Scotch, Norwegian, English and Danish. Few Americans go into this work now, although a number did in years past start out as time-keepers and have become managers. The Kanaka does not make a good manager, but if he has some one to direct him he works well, and he can learn almost any trade; of course he is at his best as a sailor, and he is such a wonderful rider that he makes an excellent cowboy.

At Waialua there is a small hospital where the labourers are treated free, and in at least one of the outlying camps there is a small cottage that is used as a dispensary. The plantation doctor has charge of the school children, vaccinating all that need it at the opening of the school year and watching them for signs of trachoma or leprosy.

Social work on plantations has not been carried on with a central organization as yet, and the welfare of the labourers depends on the attitude of the managers, who all belong to the Sugar Planters' Association. This holds yearly meetings of a week or more in Honolulu, when managers from all the Islands talk over questions pertaining to their interests.

The agricultural situation in the Islands has been carefully studied by the Bureau of Agriculture and Forestry, which reports that there are no other crops than sugar and pineapples which can be recommended as a reliable industry for the territory. This is true for several important reasons.

In the first place, from an agricultural point of view Hawaii is not a tropical country, and the strictly tropical crops do not find optimum climatic conditions. Neither has Hawaii a temperate climate, and the staple products of the temperate zone cannot be relied upon.

The distance from the mainland markets imposes a serious handicap. Moreover, both inter-island and inter-community transportation is difficult and expensive, because Hawaii is a group of comparatively small, mountainous islands with very few harbours.

It should be borne in mind, moreover, that the area of cultivated land in Hawaii is very small, the amount reclaimable still smaller, while the needs of a growing population must be met. This, of course, means intensive cultivation and a high average rate of wealth production per acre. In the ten-year period from 1900 to 1910, the population increased 24.6 per cent and the area of tillable land 3.6 per cent. The census reports also show that Hawaii is already cultivating its land far more intensively than the mainland states; for example, it supports twenty-two times as many persons per acre of improved arable land as the agricultural state of North Dakota. Clearly, the problem in Hawaii is peculiarly difficult.

It is true, also, that practically all tropical industries demand a plentiful supply of cheap labour. Labour in Hawaii is neither cheap nor plentiful. In this respect, the Islands are at a disadvantage compared with nearly all tropical countries, but much money has been spent on the industries, and the results are certainly encouraging.

How to secure cheap labour has always been a serious question for the planters. The Bureau of Immigration was established in 1876. When the Reciprocity Treaty with the United States was signed, several thousand Portuguese were sent for by the government and the planters, and many of them have remained in the country and become good citizens. About the year 1888, however, it was decided that the Chinese and the Japanese should be encouraged to come, because the cost of transportation for them was so much less. For some years the larger part of the labourers were of these two nationalities. The Japanese are still far in excess of all others, numbering over 93,000. After annexation, when the Congress of the United States prohibited immigration by the yellow races, Hawaii was obliged to seek a supply from other sources. Filipinos, of whom there are only 8,000, are next in number to the Japanese; Portuguese, Chinese, Spaniards, and Porto Ricans stand next.

After the expenses of the voyage were paid, the labourers did not always keep their agreement to work, so contract labour was introduced. Although some objections have been made to the contract system in Hawaii, it must have proved fairly satisfactory to both parties, for in those days a large number of labourers would sign a second contract on the same terms, showing at least that they were well treated and paid according to agreement.

In some cases, Chinese and Japanese labourers remained in the Islands after their contract expired, and settled there permanently. Many of the Chinese became merchants. The Portuguese went into fruit raising, and the Japanese kept mostly to the coffee plantations. In those days, the Japanese had labour unions, and they were sometimes troublesome.

Hawaii, owing to the lack of coal and iron and other minerals, can never be a manufacturing country, hence must always depend largely upon the United States for such goods. The Islands spend a large part of $60,000,000 yearly for imported articles, although, since Hawaii is a territory of the

United States, goods received from the American mainland are not classified in census returns as imports.

With the opening of the Panama Canal, the Hawaiian Islands are a necessary coaling station between the Atlantic Coast and the Far East. In anticipation of increased traffic, the harbours have been enlarged, new wharves built, a floating drydock installed, the channel widened and deepened in the harbour of Honolulu, breakwaters built at Hilo and Kahului, modern freight- and coal-handling apparatus provided, and fuel oil depots established.

CHAPTER V
IN AND OUT

Honolulu itself the traveler may perhaps be able to see in a day, with American rush, while the steamer stops on the way to Japan. To take trips on Oahu, go surf-riding, indulge in a luau, visit the plantations, and make an excursion to the volcanoes in the other islands, you must stay at least a few weeks, so that you may really see it all and have time to dream of its wonderful beauties.

Honolulu is the oldest, and so by far the most attractive, town in the Islands. Besides visits to Waikiki, the Pali, and Punchbowl, there are many delightful excursions on the island of Oahu. The Trail and Mountain Club has made excellent paths to the mountain tops, where you can get superb views. The lovely falls of Kaliuwaa are especially celebrated, while a trip to Hauula is pleasant. The coral gardens are entrancing, and near these one can see the largest wireless station in the Islands. In the great pineapple district, Wahiawa, there is a good hotel and fine bass fishing, and not far away is a big military camp.

To-day the excursion to the other islands is made fairly comfortable on the steamers of the Inter-Island Navigation Company, and one can motor to the very brink of Kilauea. But at the time of our first visit the journey was something to be endured, for the sake of the wonders at the end. The story has been often told by travelers, yet it may be worth while to recount our own experiences.

The trip certainly could not be recommended for pleasure in those days. The tiny boat was loaded down with pigs and cattle and sickly smelling sugar. The crossings were far worse than the English Channel, and our wretched little steamer reeled before the winds and tossed upon the waves. To add to our discomfort, the boat was by no means swift, and hours were consumed between the innumerable small landing-places. When we had the pleasure of stepping on solid earth once more, we found very poor hotels, if you could call them by that name, and finally, we were disappointed in the volcano itself, which was not active enough to suit us.

At our departure from Honolulu, we were quite covered with leis by the kind friends who gathered at the dock to see us off. Our boat plunged almost immediately into the high seas of the channel between Oahu and Molokai. As we passed the latter island, we had a distant view of the leper colony, on a triangle of level land, at the foot of a precipice three thousand feet high that effectually guards the patients from the landward side.

LEPER COLONY, ISLAND OF MOLOKAI.

At first the lepers resisted the attempt to banish them to the colony, and their relatives, who seemed to have no fear of the disease, concealed those who were afflicted, but this opposition decreased as the natives learned that the lepers were to be supported in comfort by the Government. They have a school, a library, newspapers, musical instruments, a theater, even moving-picture shows now, I am told—in short, everything is done to make their lives as pleasant and comfortable as possible.

Mark Twain writes of a beautiful custom in the colony. "Would you expect," he says, "to find in that awful leper settlement a custom worthy of transplanting to your own country? When death sets open the prison door of life there the band salutes the very soul with a burst of golden music."

On this island where the natives have retained their primitive habits and beliefs more than on the others of the group, the Poison God was saved at the time the idols were destroyed, a hundred years ago. It was kept here in charge of kahunas until near the end of the last century, and it is not definitely known whether it may not even now be in existence. This hideous image seems to have had the power to kill those who handled it. It has been suggested that it was made of some poisonous wood, and only the priests knew how to hold it without harm.

The boat reeled on through another rough passage to the double island of Maui, consisting of two great mountain peaks joined by a low isthmus of lava, which by degrees filled up the channel between the two original islands. We made endless stops, and by means of small boats took on and off freight, cattle, and passengers—native, Chinese and Japanese.

Our first landing was at Lahaina, once the capital of the group and the rendezvous for all the whaling ships in the Pacific. Now it is a dilapidated village, attractive only for its beautiful situation.

At Wailuku, at the northern end of the isthmus, was the home of "Father Alexander," well known as one of the early missionaries. The name Wailuku means "Water of Destruction." A great battle was fought near here by Kamehameha the Great.

Unfortunately we were unable to see the Ditch Trail, so well described by Jack London, or visit the famous Iao Valley, of which we had read such glowing descriptions. The entrance to this "gulch" is by a dark, wooded gorge that broadens out into an amphitheater surrounded by precipices as lofty as those of the Yosemite. These cliffs are covered with masses of trees, shrubs, and graceful, feathery ferns, which are veiled in turn by the mists from a thousand waterfalls. At the head of the valley stands the Needle, a natural watch-tower—of rock, but green with a luxuriant vegetation—to which the defeated army retreated in the battle of the Wailuku.

East Maui consists entirely of the huge extinct volcano of Haleakala, "house built by the sun." This, the largest extinct volcano on the surface of the globe, lifts its enormous crater, twenty miles in circumference, to the height of ten thousand feet above the sea. Some titanic eruption blew off the top of the mountain and scooped it out to the depth of two thousand feet. From the bottom of this vast cavity rise many cones—the largest a hill of seven hundred feet—and there are two great gaps in the walls, through which lava flows once made their way down to the plain. Here and there on the desert that forms the floor of the crater are scattered clumps of silversword, with long leaves shining in the sun. This plant grows only at a high altitude. Hunting for it is like hunting for the edelweiss in Switzerland. Its nearest botanical relative is found in the Himalaya Mountains. From the highest point of the rim of Haleakala these plants are said to appear about the size and brightness of silver dollars.

Glad enough we were to land at Hilo—Hawaiian for "new moon." It takes its name from the superb crescent of the bay, two miles in length, perhaps the most beautiful on the shores of the Pacific Ocean. At one end of the semicircle is Cocoanut Island, crowded with glorious palms that seem eager for the salt water, stretching their heads far out over it, as if they would drink it up. As it is on the windward side of the island, the trade winds bring Hilo a yearly rainfall of 150 inches, and the result is seen in the luxuriance of the vegetation, which nearly hides the buildings of the little city in its depths. With the bay in front, the dense forest belt in the rear, and the towering masses of Mauna Kea and Mauna Loa in the background, the situation of Hilo is glorious in its beauty.

**SILVERSWORD IN BLOOM, IN THE CRATER OF
HALEAKALA.**

On the thirty-mile trail to the crater we passed first between the brakes of
cane plantations, then through a fine tropical forest. Among the trees we
could see many gay and beautiful flowers, curious fruits and enormous tree
ferns, while in the interior were lovely glades and the little bungalows of the
coffee planters. But the island was only just being developed, so there were
numbers of ranches in the first stages of raw newness.

A search through the forests on some of the islands would disclose the
beautifully coloured landshells. These exquisite little creatures grow on the
leaves of the trees. Many of the native birds have become extinct; there
were originally seventy varieties. Game birds, however, have been
introduced from America and China, and from other countries both north
and south, including wild turkeys, quail, pheasants and ducks.

We arrived at the crater late at night, to find only a miserable hotel with a
drunken proprietor. (Liars had told us it was good.) We were forced to pass
the night there, but stayed the next day only long enough to visit the crater.

Kilauea was for us a great disappointment. It is not imposing in its
situation, lying low on the gradual slope of Mauna Loa. We had been
thrilled by pictures of the great pit of Halemaumau, the "house of
everlasting fire."[10] We had read of fountains of fire thrown a thousand feet
into the air, of great fissures from which burst clouds of deadly sulphurous
vapours, of indescribable terrors as huge billows of glowing lava surged

against the rim of the pit, of changing colours, marvelous beauty, of ropes and serpents of cooling rock in a myriad writhing and contorted shapes, of raging floods pouring down to the plain in rivers of fire from one-half to two miles in width. But alas! none of these wonders were for us. We saw only a far-stretching lake of cold, black lava, over which we could walk for miles, as safe as if we were at home. Out of a pit in the center rose a column of white vapour—which did not even smell infernal. Pele was sleeping.

FIRE HOLE, KILAUEA.

We had three days to wait in Hilo until our steamer should be ready to return to Honolulu. The hotel was a funny little one, near the sea, but we were fairly comfortable, and amused ourselves in various ways. For one thing, we tried several of the delicious tropical fruits that were to be had here—water-lemons, mangoes, papayas, mountain apples and guavas. We went on a picnic, and some one was kind enough to lend me a riding habit and a pony that had won some races. I rode astride, in native fashion. This was my first but by no means my last experience of this most natural and comfortable mode of riding. Then I had an old native woman to *lomi-lomi* me—Hawaiian for massage—as I was very lame from my long rides, and I was as much amused by her as benefited by her treatment.

We decided this was our opportunity to see a hula, and asked the coachman at the hotel to make arrangements for us at a native house. As part of the preparations, he gave the performers some wine, so the dance was in full swing when we arrived. They had made leis, which they put on us and also on themselves. A fat but good looking native woman in a holoku danced, while some others played. Another pretty native woman said she was dying to dance, but her husband, a white man, was not willing, and the last time she did it he beat her, so she did not dare to try again. It was a strange scene—the native house, the dim lights, and the wild, suggestive dance.

The trip back to Honolulu, though only two hundred miles in length, occupied two nights and a day of rough and tumble sailing, after which we were happy to get to our bungalow and Chinaman once more.

Now, the Inter-Island boats leave Honolulu twice a week for Hilo and once a week for Kona and Kau, on the lee side of the island. It is quite a different trip from that in the old days. On the way to Hilo the first landing is usually at Kawaihae, an insignificant village, of no interest except for the great heiau of Kamehameha I, the last heathen temple erected in the Islands, dating from 1791. It is over two hundred feet long and one hundred feet wide, and the walls are twelve feet thick at the base. When this temple was dedicated to the favourite war-god of the King, besides vast quantities of fruit and great numbers of hogs and dogs, eleven human beings were sacrificed on the altar.

Hilo is to-day a modern city of 10,000 people, and the shipping point for all the sugar raised on the windward side of the island. A breakwater now in process of construction will make its harbour a perfectly safe anchorage for merchant ships.

One may make the entire circuit of the island by motor from Hilo. On a branch road from the highway to Kilauea is Green Lake, an emerald-tinted sheet of water occupying an old crater. In the forest surrounding this lake the rare pink begonia, an exquisite plant, used to grow, but I am told by Mr. Castle it has become extinct.

Continuing to the southwest, the road passes through the district of Kau to Kona. Here, indeed, is the "Paradise of the Pacific." Protected from the trade winds by the huge mountain masses of Mauna Loa and Hualalai, it enjoys mild breezes from the west, which blow in from the sea all day long but give place at sunset to a wind from the mountain that cools the night. The Hawaiians have a saying that in Kona "people never die; they dry up and blow away." Daily showers toward sunset and at night keep the vegetation ever fresh and green, and make this a rich agricultural region.

Honaunau, in Kona, contains the largest of the "cities of refuge," in the walls of which are stones weighing several tons raised as high as six feet from the ground. Within these massive walls were three large heiaus, also houses for the priests and refugees. The gates were always open, and the fugitive who had crossed the threshold was absolutely safe. Old men, women, little children, defeated soldiers, all were received here, and when once the great gods had taken them under their protection, they were safe even, when they returned to their homes.

It was on the coast of Kona, at Kaawaloa, that Captain Cook was killed by the natives. A monument has been erected there, which bears this inscription: "In Memory of the Great Circumnavigator Captain James Cook, R. N., who discovered these islands on the 18th of January, A. D. 1778, and fell near this spot on the 14th of February, A. D. 1779. This monument was erected in November, A. D. 1874, by some of his fellow countrymen."

At Kailua, a seashore village further north, is the old palace of the kings of the islands. This is far from imposing in its appearance. At this place one may watch a primitive method of shipping cattle. With their horns tied to the side of a rowboat, the poor creatures are dragged through the water to the steamer, then are hoisted on board by pulleys.

The road passes next through the Kohala district, in which the town of that name is of interest as the birthplace of Kamehameha the Great. The Kohala ditch, twenty-five miles long, brings water from the mountains to the sugar plantations, fifteen miles of the way through tunnels. One may leave the main road here and take a horseback ride along this ditch, from which one can enjoy the magnificent scenery of the Waipio and Waimanu valleys, enormous "gulches," separated by sheer precipices hundreds of feet in height.

ON THE SHORES OF KAUAI, THE "GARDEN ISLAND."

The trip to Kauai, the "Garden Island," from Honolulu, requires but a single night, but is a rough passage. At Waimea Captain Cook made his first landing on the Islands. Here, too, is the ruined fort built by a Russian trader, and over which the Russian flag was raised.

The trip through the Waimea Gulch, which is called a miniature Grand Canyon of the Colorado, rewards the traveler with magnificent scenery. At the deepest part the cliffs are 3,000 feet high and the valley is a mile in width. It is said that "in the decomposing rocks the colours are as vivid as though volcanic fires were still at work."

On the shore, at the extreme western point of the island, are the Barking Sands, a row of sand dunes. "The wind on the sands makes them rustle like silk; to slide down them produces a sound like thunder; to stamp on them makes them cry out in different cadences." Not far away is an old bathing beach, where a bath was supposed to bring good luck.

At Hanalei River is one of the most ancient of the deep-water fish ponds. According to an old tradition, this was built in a single night by Menehunes, a mythical race of dwarfs, who were noted for their industry and mechanical skill and their feats of engineering.

Everywhere one is struck by the preponderance of Japanese among the inhabitants. Since this great war broke out, Japan has taken from Germany the Ladrone Islands, just north of Guam, on the way to the Philippines. She has also taken the Marshall Islands, which bring her outposts fifteen hundred miles nearer to the Pacific coast of America. If we are inclined to be a bit pessimistic over the future fate of Hawaii, perhaps a piece of recent news from Nippon may encourage us.

Japan has just passed a law permitting Japanese to become American citizens. As nearly half the present inhabitants of the Islands are Japanese and 4,000 Japanese children are born there in a year, this is an interesting consideration when difficulties between Japan and America are talked of. The Japanese-American Citizens' Association was organized by a few Japanese who are citizens by right of birth, and has grown to a membership of more than fifteen hundred. It takes an interest in municipal affairs, discusses the questions of the day, and teaches young Hawaiian-born Japanese the principles and duties of good citizenship. Rev. S. Sokabe, of Honolulu, gives its members the following advice:

"Hawaiian-born Japanese have a great mission to-day. The Japanese of Hawaii must become the pacificators should trouble come between Japan and America.... You owe it to yourselves to do this. Learn to be good American citizens, and then you will be able to help in case of trouble. You can do more to keep peace than ambassadors and ministers.... If trouble should come with Japan, you must remember that you are the sons of the President, not the sons of the Emperor."

Under the old Japanese law Japanese born in Hawaii were still subjects of Japan. Under the law lately enacted by the Diet and House of Peers of Japan, which went into effect June 1, 1916, all Japanese born in a foreign country have the right at the age of fifteen to decide whether they will become subjects of Japan or of the country of their birth; they must, however, first get the consent of their parents before giving up their citizenship in Japan.

Patriotic Americans should no longer think of Hawaii as she was eighteen years ago at the time of annexation. Then the Japanese labourer on the sugar plantations was an alien and un-American. Now he is a factor and his children a greater factor in the American civilization of the Pacific!

Moreover, to show how American and patriotic most of the islanders are, I give an account of the celebration of Washington's Birthday, when a splendid parade took place. It included the military and naval forces of the Islands, as well as Hawaiians, Chinese and Japanese—all helping to make it a success.

The native police led the procession on horseback. In quick succession the troops of the cavalry rode by, saluting the Governor as they passed the reviewing stand. The First Field Artillery followed, with their guns. Then the "Dough Boys"—as the infantry men are called—companies from the Second and the Twentieth United States Infantry; after these came the bluejackets from the four United States warships lying in the harbour, with their field pieces, each manned by a gun crew; then the marines and the Red Cross brigade. The cadets of the school for young Hawaiians and the National Guard of Hawaii presented a fine military appearance.

One of King Kalakaua's descendants, Prince Kuhio, and his brother's son, little Prince Kalakaua, were among the leaders; also the so-called Island Princesses, all on horseback. They were chosen to represent the five large islands, and had escorts of young girls on horseback dressed in the pau, followed by some lively cowboys on ponies.

Then came the floats, from which confetti were thrown. One float represented an elaborate tableau of a battle between the new Chinese republic and the old Manchu dynasty. Some took the part of the new army with their modern uniforms, and others in the old costumes lay very realistically dead behind their guns.

As evening came on the Japanese people began to assemble in the park down in the Oriental quarter, and from there marched to the palace grounds, then past the four American battleships at the docks, where they gave their *banzai* for the sailors, and were given in return a hearty American "three cheers," showing the good feeling between the two countries.

In view of the strategic value of the Islands, which, for more than fifty years, American naval officers have endeavoured to impress upon our Government, it is pleasant to learn of the loyalty and whole-hearted Americanism of the people of Hawaii. If Oahu, Guam and the Panama Canal are well fortified and sufficient numbers of troops and warships are stationed at these posts they will protect our Pacific coast better than any number of harbour defenses.

And now, with the banzai of these newest Americans ringing in our ears, we must say our "*Aloha,*" to these dream Islands, almost too perfect to be real. We say farewell, but the Spell of Hawaii will always be upon us.

THE PHILIPPINES

THE PHILIPPINES

CHAPTER I
MANILA AS WE FOUND IT

High on the bridge of the Pacific Mail Steamer *Siberia* we stood as we passed through the Boca Chica—the narrow channel—into the historic waters of Manila Bay. On one side was the mountainous island of Corregidor, rising steeply out of the sea and masking in its tropic growth many batteries and guns, on the other was the splendid mountain, Mariveles, and in the distance fine ranges rising from the sparkling ocean. Far away on the horizon, across the huge bay, lay Manila, the capital of the Philippine Islands.

Three weeks before we had left Hawaii, two days later we had steamed by Midway Island. Then we passed a few days in Japan, and coasted along the superb island of Formosa, rightly named "the beautiful"—where great mountains dipped down into the still sea—and now we were entering the Philippines, the real objective point of the official party—there were eight of us—in which we were so fortunate as to be included. We were at last going to see the interesting results of Spanish rule for three centuries, upon which were being grafted all the energy and scientific and social knowledge of the twentieth-century American.

Although both Hawaii and the Philippines are under American rule, they are like different worlds. The Land of the Palm and Pine is a much bigger problem for the United States than Hawaii. The latter is nearer home, a smaller group of islands, and is quite Americanized. It is the commercial hub of the Pacific, an important coaling station, an outlying protection for the California coast. The natives are of Polynesian extraction and American education; they are quite unlike the Filipinos in character, who are Malaysian and have had centuries of Spanish influence. The Filipinos clamour for independence, the Moros and the wild tribes must be carefully handled, while the Hawaiian is contented with his lot. Besides the necessity of maintaining an army in the Philippines so far from home, one hundred and one other difficulties are to be considered. With these facts in mind, we looked forward to interesting experiences in the Islands, and we were not disappointed.

As we approached Manila, some small scout boats, all flag bedecked, came out and joined us, and fell in behind in procession, then larger boats, one bringing the excellent Constabulary Band, which played gaily. Another, which had officials on board, exchanged greetings with us across the water, and others with unofficial people added their welcome. Quarantine was made easy, and all difficulties with customs officials were spared us. When we reached the dock it was massed with the people who had landed from the boats and with crowds from the town.

GOVERNOR GENERAL CAMERON FORBES.

At once Governor General Cameron Forbes came on board to greet the Secretary of War, and then followed a reception, the guests ranging from the apostolic delegate in his robes, the consular officials and insular officers, and the army and navy in spotless gold-braided uniforms, to the leading citizens, very intelligent looking and well mannered, and members of the Assembly. The dock was lined with troops, who paid the military honours.

After the reception on shipboard the Secretary and Mrs. Dickinson and the official members of the party were whirled off in autos, with a squadron of cavalry clattering along as escort. Another motor was waiting for us, and we soon joined the procession as it moved to the palace.

We were much interested in the sights in the streets. There were numbers of *carromatos*, little covered two-wheeled carriages, drawn by stocky Filipino ponies. The streets in this part of the town are wide, and the houses have overhanging balconies, in Spanish style. In honour of the Secretary, the buildings were draped with flags. Near the wharf the land had lately been filled in, and great docks were in construction. There was a new boulevard near the old Luneta, and an avenue named after President Taft, besides a big hotel and a hospital that had then just been finished. The harbour was filled with vessels, electric cars were running, and autos were to be seen, so at first it all looked quite up to date, until you met a carabao slowly swaying down the street, hitched to a two-wheeled cart, with a brown boy in red trousers, *piña* shirt and a big straw hat sitting on his back—"carry boy," as Secretary Dickinson named the animal. The "carry boys" do not like white people, and sometimes charge them, stamping and goring them with their

- 68 -

horns, but a small Filipino boy seems to have perfect control of them, and if they are allowed occasionally to wade in a puddle, which cools them off, they do not "go *loco*," or crazy.

It was in the palace of Malacañan, or Government House, as it is sometimes called, that Secretary and Mrs. Dickinson and ourselves stayed with the Governor General. This is a large, rambling structure in a garden by the Pasig River. Under the porte-cochère we entered a stone hall, off which were offices, then went up a long flight of stairs to a big hall looking into a court. This hall was hung with oil paintings of Spanish governors, quite well done by native artists, and in the center stood a huge one-piece table of superb *nara* wood, covered with gleaming head-axes and spears, *bolos*, *krisses*, *campilans*, and *lantankas*, used by the wild tribes and Moros.

Our rooms were large and empty, as was the entire palace—indeed, so are all the houses on account of the heat. The polished floors, too, are made of huge planks, sometimes of such valuable tropical woods as rosewood and mahogany, and are left bare. It took a little time to accustom ourselves to the hard beds with rattan bottoms, covered only by two sheets. They were carved and four-posted, and draped with mosquito netting. Two little brown lizards squeaked at us in a friendly manner, and crept down the walls, out of curiosity, no doubt, little ants kept busily crawling across the room in a line, and the mosquitoes that hid in my clothes in the rack during the daytime buzzed about at night. The heat was great, notwithstanding the electric fan, but the sliding screens that formed the sides of the room gave us some relief. These shutters are like Japanese *shoji*, made of small panes of an opalescent shell to soften the intensity of tropic sunlight, with green slit bamboo shades pulled halfway down.

When I used to write or read I sat on my rattan bed under the mosquito netting; there I could look out of the parted sides of the house to the red hibiscus border of the garden stretching along the narrow Pasig. Boatmen, in conical straw hats, perched at the ends of their *bancas*, paddled the hollowed-out logs rapidly through the water, or floated idly by, smoking their cigarettes; these boats were loaded to the gunwale with green grasses, and had canopies of matted straw. Launches, too, came chugging past, towing the big high poops covered with straw-screened *cascos*. Over beyond the river was a flat all in a green tangle, with the thatched *nipa* houses on their stilts. For the palace stands outside the more thickly settled parts of the city, which in turn surround the walled town.

The Pasig River

Manila to-day is a curious mixture of native *nipa* shacks and old Spanish churches and forts with the up-to-date American buildings and improvements. There are the different quarters, as in all cities of the Orient—Chinese, native and so on—and each has its own distinctive sights. The street smells, which are never lacking in a city, reminded us of India.

The walled city has picturesque gates breaking through the old gray battlements—the massive wall was begun in 1590—and ancient sentry houses at the corners, while behind rise the white balconies of old convents and monasteries, and buildings now used for government purposes, and towers of churches. The old moats have been filled up for sanitary reasons and are being made into wide sweeps of lawn and flower gardens, and the famous Malecon, the drive beneath the city walls, which was once upon the sea front, has been removed too far inland by the filling of the harbour to retain its old charm.

"Intramuros" (within the walls) more than half the land belongs to the Church, and church buildings abound. These are really inferior, compared with those we saw in Mexico, but some of them are very old. The Augustinian Church, finished in 1605, has enormously thick walls and a stone crypt of marvelous strength.

In the center of the town is Plaza McKinley, but the main business street is the narrow Escolta, made to look still narrower by the overhanging second stories of the buildings.

We visited the botanical gardens, a shaded park with winding paths beneath acacias and mango trees. We drove, too, through the narrow streets of the suburb of San Miguel, where we looked into tangled gardens of tropical plants, behind which were houses with broad verandas and wide-opening sides, covered by a wonderful screen of a sort of mauve morning glory, which blooms, however, all day long.

The native houses are built of bamboo with braided grass walls and thatched roofs, and are raised on stilts because of the rainy season. We went to order some embroidery one day of a Tagalog woman. Climbing a ladder into a small house, we saw the whole family sitting on the floor, working over a long frame. In some of these shacks they have a small room for visitors, with chairs and a table, and cheap prints of the Virgin on the walls. Under the house are kept usually a pig and a pony. One woman was very successful—she not only had waist patterns to show and to sell, but had a standing order from Marshall Field, in Chicago. We also visited a still more prosperous embroidery house, built of stucco, with a courtyard. These people were Spanish *mestizos*.

A visit to the cigarette factory to which we were taken by Mr. Legarda showed us one of the characteristic industries of the city and gave us an idea of the deftness and quickness of those who are employed in this work. The little women who pack the cigarettes can pick up a number of them and tell in a twinkle by the feeling just how many they hold, and the cigar wrappers work with greatest rapidity and sureness and make a perfect product. It was all very clean and fresh, with hundreds of employees in the large, airy rooms. A band played as we went through the building, and we had a generous luncheon and received innumerable presents from the managers.

Opportunity was given us for sundry little exploring trips into the suburbs of Manila.[11] We rode on horseback, in company with Secretary Dickinson, Governor Forbes and General Edwards, among little native shacks, through overgrown lanes beyond the city, and along the beach, where we saw fishermen's huts and men mending their nets, to the Polo Club. The Governor, who was most generous in giving money of his own to benefit the Islands, not only built the clubhouse and laid out the field at his own expense, but even imported Arabian horses and good Western ponies. This club is a fine thing to keep army officers in good condition and give them exercise and amusement, as well as to bring good horses into the Islands. The clubhouse, of plaited grasses, bamboo and wood, is on the edge of the beach, from which one can see the beautiful sunsets across the bay and catch the faint line of the mountains in the distance. It all seemed very far-away and tropical and enchanting.

The English-speaking residents of Manila have various other clubs, among which the Army and Navy, the English, and the University are perhaps the most important. The Officers' Club, at Fort McKinley (seven miles from Manila) has a superb situation, commanding a fine view of the mountains.

As we landed in Manila early Sunday morning, we were in time for service in the Episcopal cathedral, which had just been built. This is a handsome building in the Spanish style, large and airy, with an effective altar. It was erected by an American friend of Bishop Brent, the Episcopal bishop, who has done fine work in the Islands. According to a story that is related of this good man, he made a journey at one time into the interior of Luzon, where he found the natives sadly in need of instruction in ways of personal cleanliness. As soon as he reached the mail service again, he wrote to America for a ton of soap, which was duly shipped to him and used for the purification of the aborigines.

I was glad to visit also Bishop Brent's orphan school, consisting principally of American-mestizo children. The native women, when deserted by their white lovers, generally marry natives, who often ill-treat these half-white children, and sometimes sell them as slaves. Miss Sibley, of Detroit, was in charge of this school, which was in a big, comfortable house near the native shacks on the edge of the town, and had twelve pupils at that time.

A convent of Spanish nuns on a small island in the river, interested me greatly. It was then under the supervision of the government, for it was at that time not only a convent but also a poorhouse, a school for orphans, an asylum for insane men and women, and a reformatory for bad boys. The embroidery done at the convent was better than that made by the natives in their houses, as the thread used was finer. The nuns charged more than the natives, but they would also cut and sew, thus finishing the garments. Articles embroidered by native women were never made up by them, but had to be taken to a Chinese tailor.

The linen must first be bought, however, so I tried to do a little shopping in the city, but found it very unsatisfactory. The shops are poor, and, as one traveler has said, you can get nothing you want in them, but plenty of things you don't want, for which you can pay a very high price.

One day I was taken to a cockpit, where a cockfight was to come off. This is one of the characteristic amusements of the Filipinos, which they have engaged in since the year 1500. It is so popular that it would be difficult to put a stop to it all at once, but it has been restricted by the government to Sundays and legal holidays, which is something of a victory. (They are also passionately fond of horse racing, in regard to which other restrictions have been made.) Outside, beggars, old and blind, were crawling over the ground; natives strolled around, petting their birds, which they carried under their arms; and vendors with dirty trays of sweetmeats wandered about. We bought our tickets and passed into the rickety amphitheater.

Cocks were crowing, and such a howling as went on, the audience all looking toward us as we entered. It seemed as if they were angry with us for stepping into the arena, and yet there was no other way to reach the seats. Our guides pointed to a shaky ladder that led into a gallery, but we preferred to sit far back in the chairs about the pit. There were natives, Chinese, and mestizos present. We soon discovered that they were not angry with us, but we had entered at a moment when the betting was going on, and the cocks in the ring were so popular that there was great excitement.

Each cock was allowed to peck the neck of the other and get a taste of blood, while they were still held under their owners' arms. The fighting cocks did not look quite like ours. They were armed for the fray with sharp "slashers" attached to their spurs. When the betting had subsided the cocks were left to themselves in the ring, and they generally went for each other at once. What a hopping and scuttling! Feathers flew, the crowd cheered, and the cocks went at each other again and again until they were hurt or killed. The referee then decided upon the victor. Sometimes the cocks did not seem to interest the crowd, and then their owners would take them out of the ring before fighting; at times the cocks refused to fight. It was not so exciting as I had expected, and when we considered that the birds were to be eaten anyway, it did not seem so cruel and terrible as I thought it would.

Speaking of cocks being eaten, the principal foods of the Filipinos are fowls and eggs, as well as rice, fish and carabao meat, but as the "carry-boys" are good workers they are not often eaten. Pigs are kept by the Filipinos, and are put on a raised platform for about six weeks before killing, so as to keep them clean and fatten them with good food. Salads, crawfish and trout, as well as cocoanut milk, red wine and wild coffee, are among the things they live on. Army people in the Islands often have, in addition, wild deer and wild boar which are shot by the American officers, besides excellent game birds, such as the minor bustard, jungle fowl, wild chicken, quail, snipe and duck.

MALACAÑAN PALACE.

I was asked to receive with the Secretary and Mrs. Dickinson and General and Mrs. Edwards, at the Governor General's reception at Malacañan, where we stood in line and shook hands with some seventeen hundred persons. It was a remarkable scene. The palace, which opens up handsomely, and the terrace overhanging the river, were outlined by a myriad electric lights, while launches came and went with guests, and the Philippine Constabulary Band played in the interior court. The papal delegate was there in his canonicals, with his accompanying monsignors, and barefooted friars in cowls. There were foreign consuls in their uniforms, and many Filipina women, with pretty manners and dainty ways, some in their native dress, which is so quaint and gaily coloured. Insurrecto generals came, too, who looked like young boys, and members of the high courts, very wise and dignified.

After most of the guests had arrived, there was a *rigodon* of honour, in which all took part. The rigodon is the dance of the Filipinos, and of so much importance to them that it was considered essential that the Secretary and his party should be able to join in it. Accordingly, we had all practised it on the ship before reaching Manila. It is said that ex-President Taft won much of his way into the hearts of these island people by his skill and evident delight in this dance, which is something like a graceful and dignified quadrille, with much movement and turning.

To show that traveling in an official party is not "all play and no work," I may just note the program carried out by the men on the day following this reception. Rising at six o'clock and taking an early breakfast, they went on board the commanding general's yacht and cruised across Manila Bay to visit the new defenses on the island of Corregidor, which rises a sheer five hundred feet out of the water. For hours they moved from one place to another in the heat, inspecting huge guns and mortars and barracks and storehouses, all hidden away so as not to be seen from the sea, although great gashes in the cliffs showed where the trolley roads and the inclined planes ran. It is really the key to our possessions in the Far East. Thousands of men were working like ants all over the place. It was two o'clock before the party reached the tip-top, where they had a stand-up luncheon at the quarters of the commanding officer. Then they came back to the yacht, and fairly tumbled down just wherever they happened to be for a siesta. They were then taken to Cavite, ten miles away, which is one of the two naval stations. There they landed again and visited the picturesque old Spanish fortifications and the quarters.

A *baile*, or ball, was given in honour of the Secretary by the Philippine Assembly, at their official building, where all the ladies of our party wore the Filipina dress. This is ordinarily made of piña cloth, a cheap, gauzy material, manufactured from pineapple fiber. The waist, called *camisa*, is made with winglike sleeves and a stiff kerchief-like collar, named *panuela*. The skirt may be of any material, quite often a handsome brocade, and among the Tagalogs a black silk open-work apron finishes the costume. The white suits and uniforms of the men and the bright-coloured dresses made this ball a gay and lively scene. The band played incessantly, and after the Secretary and Mrs. Dickinson had stopped receiving at the head of the stairs, there was a rigodon, which we all danced in as stately a manner as we could. But my most vivid recollection of the ball is of the heat and the pink lemonade, which poisoned a hundred people and made me deadly ill all that night.

MRS. ANDERSON IN FILIPINA COSTUME.

The Governor General gave a big dinner for the Secretary of War at the palace one evening. We assisted also at the opening of the new theater—which is called the finest in the Far East—at which Marshall Darrach gave recitations from Shakespeare. I must not forget the gala performance at the new theater, too, which was arranged by the society people of the city. All the performers were amateurs, so we rather dreaded the evening, which promised to be interminable, but everything was so good that the time passed quickly. The little ladies sang quite acceptably, and played the violin and the piano; and a lot of tiny tots, children of the best people, gave an amusing vaudeville that really was exceedingly funny and was much applauded. We could hardly believe that it was all amateur.

The Government Dormitory for Girls, which we visited, I found most interesting. There were one hundred and fifty, eight sleeping in each room.

These girls came from different provinces all over the Islands. As there are so many distinct dialects, some of them could understand one another only in English, and no other language is allowed to be spoken. One of the girls made a speech in English welcoming the Secretary and did it extremely well. Having learned, among other things, to cook, they gave us delicious tea and cakes and candies on a half-open veranda among the vines and Japanese lanterns. Some were taking the nurses' course, which seemed to be the most popular. These pretty girls danced for us in their stiff, bright-coloured costumes, swaying and waving their hands, and turning and twirling in their languid but dignified manner. It appeared to be a mixture of a Spanish and a native dance, and was altogether quite charming.

A morning with Mr. Worcester at the Bureau of Science was most delightful. This bureau is so much more than a museum of scientific specimens that I cannot begin to do justice to it in a single paragraph. It was started at first as a Bureau of Government Laboratories in charge of the chemical and biological work of the government, the departments of zoölogical and botanical research were subsequently added, and finally the Bureau of Ethnology and the Bureau of Mines were incorporated with it. Not only were all these departments coördinated under one head, preventing overlapping and securing economy and efficiency of administration, but this work was correlated with that of the Philippine General Hospital and the College of Medicine and Surgery. When this comprehensive plan was formed all the scientific work of the government was carried on in "a hot little shack," and the scheme was commonly referred to as "Worcester's Dream," but at the time of our visit the dream had come true. The departments were manned by thoroughly trained men from the States, and the Bureau of Science was one of the world's greatest scientific institutions.

The Philippine Bureau of Science "is now dead." When the Democratic Administration took charge it was announced that all theoretical departments, such as ethnology, botany, ornithology, photography and entomology (!) were to be "reduced or eliminated." It was afterward made plain that all work which was considered practical would be continued, but the mischief had been done, the men who made the institution had left, and under present conditions it is impossible to secure others who are equally competent in their place. Our only consolation is to be derived, as Mr. Worcester himself says, "from contemplating the fact that pendulums swing."

Though so recently established, the museum contained in 1910 a wonderful exhibit of the plants and animals of the Islands. We took a peep into the butterfly room, where we admired some rare and lovely ones with a feathery velvet sheen the colour of the sea. We saw also the huge brown

Atlas moth touched with coral, like a cashmere shawl, with eyes of mother-of-pearl on his wings. We noticed that the females were larger than the males, and even those of the same variety often differed greatly in colour. In one case a female was big, and brown and violet in colour, while her mate was small, and blue and yellow.

In the next room were beetles, some of which were like the matrix of turquoise, and others had shimmering, changeable shades of green and bronze. There were beetles like small turtles, and long, horned beetles like miniature carabaos.

Afterward we visited the birds. Bright-coloured sun birds, with long beaks, which feed on the honey of flowers; clever tailor birds, small and brown, with green heads and gray breasts, which sew leaves together with vegetable fiber to make their nests; birds of whose nests the Chinese make their famous soup, and the blue kingfishers, of whose brilliant feathers these same Chinese make jewelry; fire-breasted birds, too, and five-coloured birds. There were birds that build their nest four feet or more under the ground, and hornbills, that wall up their wives in holes in the trees while they are hatching their eggs, the males bringing them food and dropping it through a small opening. There, too, I saw the fairy bluebird.

Near by, we visited an orchid garden, and passed under gates and bamboo trellises dripping with every kind of orchid. The Philippines are the paradise of these remarkable plants, and many are the adventures that collectors of them have had in the interior of these Islands.

Then we passed into the Jesuit chapel and museum. We were greeted at the door by several black-robed priests, who smiled and bowed and talked all at once. They escorted us first to the museum, where there were cases of shells—heart-shaped shells, trumpet shells, scalloped shells big enough for a bathtub—all kinds of shells, and the paper nautilus, which is not a shell but an egg case. Then there were land shells, polished red and green, Venus' flower baskets, exquisite glass sponges, corals of all kinds—fine branches of the red and the white—and an enormous turtle that weighed fifteen hundred pounds.

In the cases at the side of the room were animals of the country—flying monkeys, with sucking pads on their toes to help them climb the trees, big, furry bats and flying lizards. A tiny buffalo, which was discovered only a few years ago up in the hills, and a small spotted deer were in the collection. A big monkey-catching eagle, white and brown, was here, and the paroquet that carries leaves for her nest in her red tail, as well as a pigeon with ruffs of green and blue about her neck, and a bald crown, which was caused, the natives say, by flying so high that her head hit the sky.

Numerous entertainments and receptions were crowded into that too short visit to Manila. July 25th had been declared a national holiday. A musical program was given in honour of the Secretary by five thousand Manila school children. One afternoon Mrs. Dickinson received some of the Filipina ladies, who sang and played on the piano quite well.

Another day the officers and ladies at Fort McKinley entertained the party at luncheon at the Officers' Club. Before luncheon there was a military review in which the troops from all over the islands participated, followed by some good shell firing out in the chaparral, as under war conditions, and a display of wireless work. A special drill was given by Captain Tom Anderson—the son of General Anderson—whose company was one of the best drilled in the army, and went through the manual and marching with only one order given, counting to themselves in silence the whole seventeen hundred counts, all in perfect unison.[12]

In the Secretary of War's speech that afternoon he took occasion to say, "General Duvall, you have not said too much in favour of the Army. You have not overdrawn the picture, for a steadier moving column or brighter eyed men and a more soldierly set of men I have never seen anywhere."

The reception by General and Mrs. Duvall was a brilliant affair, chiefly of the army and navy. The handsome house with its wide verandas stood in a garden overlooking Manila Bay.

On the Luneta there was, one evening, the largest gathering that had assembled on that historic plaza since the days of the "Empire," for the Secretary of War was expected to be there. The people hoped that he brought with him a proclamation of immediate independence to be announced at that time. The Luneta had once been at the edge of the water, but a great space had been filled in beyond it, and buildings were going up—a large hotel, which would make all the difference in the world to tourist travel in the Philippines, and a huge Army and Navy Club—so that it was planned to remove the Luneta farther out some day, again to the water's edge. On this particular evening, the oval park was crowded with picturesque people, almost all the men in white, the soldiers in their trig khaki, and the women in their gaily coloured dresses and panuelas. Rows of carriages circled round and round, as the two bands played alternately. After a time we left our automobiles and walked in the throng. A magnificent sunset was followed by the gorgeous tints of the afterglow, and dusk came on and evening fell while we watched and were watched. Soon a thousand electric lights, that were carried in rows around the plaza and over the kiosks of the bands, sparkled out in the darkness. The beauty of the scene, the animation of the crowd, driving or walking in groups, and the refreshing coolness after the heat of the day, made this a lasting memory.

CHAPTER II
THE PHILIPPINES OF THE PAST

How have the Philippines come to present such a unique combination of Spanish and Malay civilization? Let us look into their past. We find for the early days myths and legends, preserved by oral tradition. Two quaint stories told by the primitive mountain people, which show how they believe the Islands first came into being and how the first man and woman entered into this world, are worth transcribing for their naïve simplicity:

"A long time ago there was no land. There were only the sea and the sky. A bird was flying in the sky. It grew tired flying. It wanted something to rest upon. The bird was very cunning. It set the sea and sky to quarreling. The sea threw water up at the sky. The sky turned very dark and angry. Then the angry sky showered down upon the sea all the Islands. That is how the Islands came."

This second tale is even more child-like:

"A great bamboo grew on one of the Islands. It was very large around, larger than any of the others. The bird lit on the ground and began to peck the bamboo. A voice inside said, 'Peck harder, peck harder.' The bird was frightened at first, but it wanted to know what was inside. So it pecked and pecked. Still the voice said, 'Peck harder, peck harder.' At last a great crack split the bamboo from the bottom to the top. Out stepped a man and a woman. The bird was so frightened that it flew away. The man bowed very low to the woman, for they had lived in different joints of the bamboo and had never seen each other before. They were the first man and woman in the world."

These natives believe there are good and evil spirits, and they invoke the agency of the latter to explain the mystery of death. They say the first death occurred when the evil spirit lightning became angry with man and hurled a dangerous bolt to earth.

The first suggestion of real history is found in the traditions that tell of Malays from the south who came and settled on these islands. It is said a race of small black people were already here—the Negritos—who resembled the African negroes, and who retired into the hills before the invaders.

Next we hear of a Mohammedan priest who came to the southern Philippines and gave the people his religion. His followers have to this day been called Moros.

It was more than two centuries before Captain Cook visited Hawaii, that white men discovered the Philippines. Magellan, the famous Portuguese navigator, while sailing in the service of Spain, landed on Mindanao and Cebu, and took possession of the group in the name of the Spanish king. Before starting from Seville on this voyage around the world, Magellan had already spent seven years in India and sailed as far as Sumatra, so he already knew this part of the world. This time he was in search of the Spice Islands and of a passage from the Atlantic to the Pacific Ocean. He had touched first at Teneriffe and then crossed the Atlantic to Brazil, making his way along the coast of South America. There were many hardships and difficulties to contend with, and mutiny in the fleet resulted in several deaths. But, as we all know, he persevered, and on the 15th of October, 1520, discovered the straits which were named after him.

The Ladrones were reached after fourteen tedious weeks, and on St. Lazarus' day, in 1521, the Philippines were sighted and named by him for the saint. In the early times they were sometimes referred to by the Spaniards as the Eastern, and later as the Western, Islands. They were finally named the Philippines by Ruy Lopez de Villalobos, after his king, Philip the Second.

Magellan was quite unlike Captain Cook, whose visit to Hawaii has been mentioned. He was a nobleman and full of the religious enthusiasm that fired the Spaniards of his day. He was accompanied by several friars, who at once began missionary work among the natives, and only a week after his arrival the Cebuan chief and his warriors were baptized into the Christian faith. Unfortunately, Magellan took sides with the Cebuans in their warfare against a neighbouring tribe, and in the battle he was killed. After his death, the same chieftain turned on Magellan's followers, but some escaped to their ships. Out of two hundred and fifty men who had set sail three years before, only eighteen, after suffering incredible hardships on the long journey by way of India and the Cape of Good Hope, returned safely to Spain.

The next explorer who touched at the Islands was the Englishman, Sir Francis Drake, of Spanish Armada fame, who sailed in 1570 on a voyage round the world. We also hear of another Briton, William Dampier, a noted free-booter, who, in 1685, tried to cross the Isthmus of Panama with Captain Sharp. Three times he sailed round the world, and touched at the northern as well as the southern Philippine Islands.

Magellan, Drake and Dampier gave the western world much knowledge of the Far East, but did not remain long enough in the Islands to have any great or lasting influence over the natives. The work of civilizing them was left to Legaspi and the Spanish friars, who were the first real settlers.

In 1565, the Philippines were occupied by an expedition under Miguel Lopez de Legaspi, *alcalde* of the City of Mexico, who was charged to open a new route to Java and the Southern Islands. On his return voyage he was to examine the ports of the Philippines, and, if expedient, to found a colony there. In any case he was to establish trade with the Islands. The viceroy of Mexico charged him that the friars with the expedition were to be treated with the utmost consideration, "since you are aware that the chief thing sought after by His Majesty is the increase of our holy Catholic faith and the salvation of the souls of those infidels."

Cebu was occupied, and Manila was taken and made the seat of government. The occupation of the Islands was not exactly by force of arms, for there was no fighting, although they found the islands well populated and the people more or less armed. The natives seemed to recognize and submit to a better government and religion than they had ever known. The reports of the Spaniards of the time speak of the success of small expeditions of perhaps a hundred men, who took over whole provinces. These soldiers were accompanied by Spanish priests, who settled among the people, preaching Christianity in the native tongues. The friars persuaded them to give up their continual feuds and submit to the central authority which the friars represented.

Legaspi brought with him from Mexico four hundred Spanish soldiers. Later eight hundred more arrived, and civilian Spaniards, both married and single, sailed to the Islands as settlers. In 1591, according to the records of Spanish grants, there were 667,612 natives under Spanish rule, and twenty-seven officials to enforce the laws and preserve order. It was reported that in a majority of the grants there was peace, justice and religious instruction. There were Augustinian, Dominican and Franciscan friars as well as secular clergy. These men were not only priests but also fighters and organizers, and did fine work for many years, until long-continued possession of power gradually made the orders corrupt and grasping.

Upon their first arrival, the Spaniards found the people established in small villages, or *barangays*, where the chief lived surrounded by his slaves and followers. It was considered wise to continue this system, ruling the villages through the local chieftain, whom the Spaniards called *cabeza de barangay*. Churches were erected, convent houses were built about them, and the natives were urged to gather near by. It was ordered that "elementary schools should be established, in which the Indians will be taught not only Christian doctrine and reading and writing but also arts and trades, so that they may become not only good Christians but also useful citizens."

So at the end of the sixteenth century the Philippines were at peace. The natives were allowed to move from one town to another, but they were required to obtain permission, in order to prevent them from wandering about without religious instruction. The tendency of the Malays is to separate into small groups, and they have never been dwellers in large towns. The Spanish priests, therefore, found a constant effort necessary to keep them concentrated about the churches "under the bells."

"UNDER THE BELLS."

The fervour of religious reform which started in Germany was followed by an equal fervour within the Roman Catholic Church. The period of Julius II and Leo X was over; the Council of Trent had met. Ignatius Loyola had seen his visions and sent forth his company, and Spain was full of priests eager to serve God with the same stern energy which the previous generation had shown in the search for lands and gold and fabulous gems. No duty was so grave as that of conformity to the Church, no stigma so galling as that of heretic. To convert the heathen was an obligation binding upon all men. All Spanish colonies were missions; the Philippines were always rather a mission than a colony.

Until the revolt of 1896, Spain never found it necessary to hold the Islands by armed force; her dominion there was based rather on her conquest of the minds and souls of men. There had been a few uprisings, however, and early in the eighteenth century a Spanish governor and his son were murdered by a mob. But notwithstanding occasional difficulties, in the main there was peace until the civil service of the Philippines was assimilated with that of Spain. Then officials became dependent upon their supporters at home, and were changed with every change of the ministry.

Some Spaniard writing at the time said that with the opening of the Suez Canal Spanish office holders descended on the Islands like locusts.

At the end of the nineteenth century, the Spanish army had grown to 17,859 of all ranks, only 3,005 of whom were Spaniards, and there was a constabulary of over 3,000 officers and men, who were almost entirely natives. The rule of Spain was secured by a native army. There could have been no widespread discontent, or that army would not have remained true to its allegiance, especially as its recruits were obtained by conscription.

The chronicles remind us, however, that the Spaniards did not have things all their own way. In the early days, they were at first friendly with the Chinese, and Mexico carried on a flourishing trade with China by way of Manila until the pirate Li Ma Hong raided the Islands. The Spaniards were on good terms with the Japanese until the latter massacred the Jesuit friars in Japan. When the Shogun Iyeyasu expelled the priests he sent away even those who were caring for the lepers, and as a final insult, he sent to Manila three junks loaded with lepers, with a letter to the governor general of the Philippines, in which he said that, as the Spanish friars were so anxious to provide for the poor and needy, he sent him a cargo of men who were in truth sore afflicted. Only the ardent appeals of the friars saved these unfortunates and their contaminated vessels from being sunk in Manila Bay. Finally the governor yielded, and these poor creatures were landed and housed in the leper hospital of San Lazaro, which was then established for their reception and which remains to-day.

The Spanish governors were also hampered by the lack of effective support from the older colony of Mexico, which was so much nearer than the home land that they naturally turned to it for aid. One of them wrote pathetically to the King of Spain:

"And for the future ... will your Majesty ordain that Mexico shall furnish what pertains to its part. For, if I ask for troops, they send me twenty men, who die before they arrive here, and none are born here. And if I ask for ammunition, they laugh at me and censure me, and say that I ask impossible things. They retain there the freight money and the duties; and if they should send to this state what is yours, your Majesty would have to spend but little from your royal patrimony."

The Portuguese were a source of anxiety to the colonists until Portugal fell into the hands of Spain. The Dutch, too, who were growing powerful in the Far East, even took Formosa, which brought them altogether too near, but they were driven out of that island by the great Chinese pirate Koxinga.[13]

From the time of Legaspi to the end of Spanish rule there were occasional attacks upon the Chinese residing in the archipelago, who were never allowed to live in the Islands without exciting protest and dislike, based partly upon religious, partly upon commercial grounds. During the last one hundred years of Spanish supremacy, the greatest danger to their power was the presence of the Chinese. Efforts to exclude them were never effective or long enduring, and yet it was felt that the men who came as labourers and traders were the advance guard of an innumerable host. In business the Malay has never been the equal of the shrewd Chinaman, and although the latter might be converted and take a Spanish name, yet it was always gravely suspected that a search would find joss sticks smoldering in front of the tutelary deity of commerce hidden behind the image of the Virgin in his chapel.

So the Chinaman, like the Jew in medieval Europe, carried on his trade in constant danger of robbery and murder. This antipathy did not, however, extend to Filipina women, many of whom married the foreigners. Among the leaders in the Filipino insurrection against the United States, Aguinaldo, two of his cabinet, nine of his generals, and many of his more important financial agents were of Chinese descent.

In 1762 the English swooped down upon Manila, but they held the capital only two years, for, by the Treaty of Paris, the lands they had taken were returned to Spain. It is said the English conquest, brief as it was, brought good results to the Islands.

Before going on to the struggle against the friars, I wish to quote from my father's letters describing his experiences in the Philippines twenty years before American occupation.

"At Sea, December 2, 1878.

"Yesterday I left Manila, where I have been since the 6th of last month.... Our first days there were spent in firing salutes and exchanging visits, and going through all the forms which are customary when a government vessel comes into a foreign port. Admiral Patterson sent me here to settle a stabbing affray on board the American barque *Masonic*, and that took up my attention at first. In the evenings I went to the opera, and visited the sights of the city. On account of earthquakes, all the buildings are but one story high. The customs, fashions, etc., are Spanish. Every one was polite and I found it very pleasant; but, as you might expect, after a little while I grew restless. I heard that there was some beautiful scenery in the interior, and I resolved to go on an investigating trip and see it. Our vice-consul, Mr. Yongs, and another gentleman went with me.

"From Manila we went in a boat up a short river, which had its rise in a large lake, about twenty-five miles long, that we crossed in a steamer. I think I never saw such quantities of two things as were on that lake—namely, ducks and mosquitoes.

"From the lake we continued our journey in two-horse vehicles, like the *volantes* of Havana, and in these we went from village to village, on our way to the mountains. We were very well treated. The Spanish authorities at Manila provided us with whatever we required. The villages were clusters of thatched huts around a church, and the religion seemed to be a curious mixture of Roman Catholic Christianity and pagan superstition, as I concluded from the style of the pictures with which the churches were adorned. These were chiefly representations of hell and its torments. Devils, with the traditional tails and horns, and armed with pitchforks, were turning over sinners in lakes of burning brimstone....

"We found the natives very musical; they sang and played on a variety of instruments, and they were rather handsome. The women had, without exception, the longest and most luxuriant hair I ever saw in all my travels. You know it is a rare thing among us for a woman to have hair that sweeps the ground, but here the exception is the other way; nearly every woman I saw had hair between five and six feet in length.

"I was told that back among the mountains there existed tribes whom the Spaniards have never been able to conquer, and no one dares to venture among them, not even the priests. Our road was constantly ascending, and as we advanced toward the interior the scenery became beautiful. Peaks of mountains rose all about us; plains and valleys stretched out, covered with tropical vegetation; picturesque villages, clustering around their churches, were visible here and there; and in the distance were glimpses of the sea, sparkling and bright in the sun.

"I was told of a wonderful ravine among the mountains that was worth seeing and I decided to visit it, especially as it was a favourable time; the river, by which it had to be approached, was then high, and its fifteen cascades, which usually had to be climbed past, dragging the canoe, were reduced to four. I took three natives with me, and we ascended successfully. I have called it a ravine, but a gorge would be a better term, for it is worn directly through the mountain by a large river, and the rock rises up on each side, as sheer and straight as if cut by machinery.

"After I had ascended a certain distance, I stopped for a time to examine all the wild magnificence about me. The rocky wall on each side was so high that when I looked up I could see the stars shining in that bright noonday, as if it were night. Huge birds came flapping up the gorge far above my head; and yet they were far below the top of the mountain of rock. I do not know how many feet it rose, but I never saw any precipice where the impression of height was so effectually given—it seemed immense.

"Beneath us was the deep, broad stream, looking very dark in the twilight that such a shadow made, and I could not help feeling awestruck. But the opening of the gorge framed as smiling and cheerful a landscape as could possibly be devised, to contrast with the inner gloom. It was a wide, varied and splendid view of the country beyond, sloping to the distant sea, and all of it as aglow with light and colour as sea and land could be, beneath a tropic sun.

"Descending the river on our way out, I had a characteristic adventure, which will make me satisfied for a time. We had passed two of the rapids in safety, but as we approached the third, the canoe struck on a rock or something in the current, bow on, and swinging round, half filled with water. The natives in the end of the canoe nearest the rock sprang out and clung to the vines which hung over its sides, but the other man and I went over the fall in the half-swamped canoe, and were wholly at the mercy of the stream, with an unusually good prospect of getting a good deal more of it.

"The fall once passed through, the current drove us toward the shore, if that is what you would call a precipice of rock, running straight down far below the surface of the water. I succeeded in grasping the vines and pulling the canoe after me by my feet. The water was quite close by the rock, and the other two men, crawling down to us, hung on with me, and bailed out the boat till it was safely afloat, and then we went down the rest of the way without accident."

Before the middle of the last century, life in the Philippines must have been, for Spaniards and natives alike, one long period of siesta. The sound of the wars and the passing of governments and kings in Europe must have seemed to these loiterers in a summer garden like the drone of distant bees. After that period conditions changed rapidly. In 1852, the Jesuits returned to the Philippines; in 1868, the reactionary Queen Isabella II fled from Spain, because of the rise of republicanism; in 1869, the Suez Canal was opened. All these events had their influence, but the return of the Jesuits was of dominating importance.

Throughout the nineteenth century the sole idea of the Tagals was to get rid of the friars, and for several reasons, which I will explain as briefly as possible. The Roman Catholic clergy are divided into regular and secular. Members of the secular clergy are subordinate to the bishops and archbishops, through whom the decrees of the Holy See are promulgated. The regular clergy, monks and friars, are subordinate to provincials elected for comparatively short terms of office by members of their own order.

The Jesuits form a group by themselves but belong rather to the regular than the secular.

Over three hundred years after the conversion of the Filipinos, the Spanish monks and friars considered it still unsafe to admit natives into the hierarchy of the Catholic Church. *The secular clergy were mostly natives, the regular clergy were Spaniards.* Naturally this condition of affairs in time produced friction.

To understand the case in regard to the Jesuits, it is necessary to go back nearly a century. In 1767, the King of Spain issued a decree expelling the Jesuits from his possessions. Their property was confiscated, their schools were closed, and they were treated as enemies of the state. They had been among the earliest missionaries in the Philippines, and were probably the wealthiest and most influential of all the clergy there. Their departure left no priests for the richest parishes in the provinces of Cavite and Manila, which had been their sphere of influence. The question at once arose as to who would succeed them, and as it happened, the Archbishop of Manila who had to answer it was a member of the secular clergy, a Spanish priest to be sure, but of liberal tendencies. Consequently, he filled the parishes with native priests, who continued to occupy them until the return of the Jesuits.

Now the parish priest was the most influential man in the community. As native priests used this influence to build up the prestige of the seculars, the ecclesiastical feuds which arose became embittered by racial antagonism.

When a royal order was received permitting the return of the Jesuits it became at once necessary to find places for them in the ecclesiastical government. Spain decided that the parishes of Cavite and Manila should be henceforth filled by members of the order of Recollets, who were to transfer their missions in Mindanao to the Jesuits. The Archbishop protested against this increase in the power of the regular clergy, and the Governor General assembled his council to act upon the protest. All the members of the council who were born in Spain voted against the Archbishop. All those born in the Philippines voted for him. The regulars gained another victory over the seculars; the native was publicly informed that he was not fit to administer the parishes of his own people, and he saw himself definitely assigned to the position of lay brother or of curate. Whatever threads of attachment there had been between the opposing factions broke on the day of that decision, and every native priest from that moment became a center of disaffection and of the propaganda of hatred of the friars. This was perhaps the real beginning of the movement which continued, now secretly, now openly, until it broke out in actual revolt in 1872. The Spaniards put down this uprising of the Tagalogs with such cruelty that they feared a later retaliation, and sought help from the friars. This the friars gave them, in return for added wealth and power, which was granted, of course, at the expense of the vanquished natives.

Worcester writes in one of his earlier books, "During the years 1890-93, while traveling in the archipelago, I everywhere heard the mutterings that go before a storm. It was the old story: compulsory military service; taxes too heavy to be borne, and imprisonment or deportation with confiscation of property for those who could not pay them; no justice except for those who could afford to buy it; cruel extortion by the friars in the more secluded districts; wives and daughters ruined; the marriage ceremony too costly a luxury for the poor; the dead refused burial without payment of a substantial sum in advance; no opportunity for education; little encouragement for industry and economy, since to acquire wealth meant to become a target for officials and friars alike; these and a hundred other wrongs had goaded the natives and half-castes until they were stung to desperation."

The dissensions in the Philippines which ended in the rebellion of 1896-7 began with disagreements among the Spaniards themselves. A progressive party arose before which the clerical or conservative party slowly but steadily lost ground, and the legislation of modern Spain was by degrees introduced into the Islands. The country was not able to endure the taxation which would have been necessary to raise the revenues to carry out this legislation. Hence laws which were passed against the advice of the Spanish clergy in the Philippines were left largely in their hands for execution, not because they were loved or trusted, but because they were the only Spanish functionaries who knew the language and the people and whose residence in the Islands was a permanent one. If the friars had used their power wisely and unselfishly, there would have been no trouble, but they used it too often simply to keep the people down and extort money, for which they gave little return.

By degrees the mestizos took sides. The Chinese mestizos soon grew restive under this priestly government, and aided the progressive Spanish party in Manila. As time passed they had it borne in upon them that revolution might pay.

The insurrection of 1896-7 was planned and carried out under the auspices of a society local to the Philippines, called the "Katipunan," the full title of which may be translated as "Supreme Select Association of the Sons of the People." According to Spanish writers on the subject, it was the outgrowth of a series of associations of Freemasons formed with the expressed purpose of securing reforms in the government of the Philippines, but whose unexpressed and ultimate object was to obtain the independence of the archipelago. As if to accomplish this purpose, a systematic attack was made on the monastic orders in the Philippines, to undermine their prestige and to destroy their influence upon the great mass of the population. The honorary president of the Katipunan was José Rizal, whose name was used, without his permission, to attract the masses to the movement.

Rizal was born in 1861 not far from Manila. He came of intelligent stock. After his early training at the Jesuit school in Manila and the Dominican university, Rizal went to Spain, where he took high honors at the University of Madrid in medicine and philosophy. Post-graduate work in France and Germany followed.

JOSE RIZAL.

He was an ardent patriot, and in order to awaken his countrymen to the need of reform, although he was a Roman Catholic, he published while in Germany his book called "Noli Me Tangere,"—Touch Me Not—which dealt with the immoral life of the friars. An English translation has been issued with the title, "The Social Cancer." The circulation of the book in the Islands was forbidden, but it was read by most of the educated Filipinos. In reading it, one is again and again struck by the author's clear comprehension of the needs and the difficulties of the Filipinos, and the calm, unprejudiced way in which their problems are discussed.

In 1891, Rizal began the practice of medicine in Hongkong. Meanwhile, the Spanish authorities, in their desire to get him into their power, worked upon his feelings by persecuting his mother. The trick was successful, and he returned to Manila, where he was soon arrested, and banished to the island of Mindanao.

The most powerful leader of the insurrection was Andres Bonifacio, a passionate and courageous man of little education. He sent an agent to Dr. Rizal to aid him in escaping from his place of exile and to request him to lead the Katipunan in open revolt. Rizal refused, believing that the Filipinos were not yet ready for independence. Bonifacio resolved to proceed without him.

Bonifacio assured his audience that when he gave the signal the native troops would join them. It was of great importance to the success of his plan that the army, as in 1872, was engaged in operations against the Moros. There were available in Manila only some three hundred Spanish artillery, detachments amounting to four hundred men, including seamen, and two thousand native soldiers. The plot was discovered, but Bonifacio escaped from Manila, and sent out orders for an uprising in that part of Luzon which had been organized by the Katipunan. Manila was attacked, but the rebels were repulsed. Martial law was proclaimed in eight provinces of Luzon, followed by wholesale executions. Many of those arrested on suspicion "were confined in Fort Santiago, one batch being crowded into a dungeon for which the only ventilation was a grated opening at the top, and one night the sergeant of the guard carelessly spread his sleeping-mat over this, so the next morning some fifty-five asphyxiated corpses were hauled away."

Just before the outbreak, Rizal received permission to join the army in Cuba as surgeon, but on the way there was arrested and brought back to Manila. His fate was now sealed. The trial by court-martial was a farce. On a December day in 1896 he was led to execution.

FORT SANTIAGO.

Rizal was undoubtedly the noblest and most unselfish of the Filipino leaders, and his execution was not only a crime but a blunder on the part of the Spanish authorities. From his prison he issued an address to the Filipinos remarkable for its moderation and its condemnation of the "savage rebellion," stating that the education of the people must precede any truly beneficial reforms, and urging them to go back to their homes. The Spanish officials deemed this not sufficiently "patriotic" to be published, and sentenced its author to the death of a traitor by shooting in the back. To-day he is the national hero of the Filipinos.

The seacoast towns were under the leadership of Emilio Aguinaldo, a young radical, who was already a recognized leader among the local disaffected. The Spaniards had not expected this outbreak in Cavite. Aguinaldo had personally assured the governor of the province of his devotion to Spain, but when fighting began isolated Spanish officers were killed and their families carried into captivity. The difficulties, of the Spaniards were increased by the fact that the defense of Manila and Cavite until reinforcements arrived, would be largely in the hands of native troops, among whom the Katipunan was known to have been at work. But the troops of the old native regiments—the men who for years had followed Spanish officers—were on the whole faithful, and it was largely due to them that Manila and Cavite were held.

The leaders in the insurrection were of that class who called themselves *ilustrados*, enlightened, a class whose blood is, in almost every case, partly Spanish or partly Chinese. The supremacy of the friars was passing, and men of this class intended to be the heirs to their domain. The idea of forming a republic and even of adopting the titles appropriate to a republic to designate the functionaries of a Malay despotism was an afterthought.

Reinforcements arrived from Spain, and by June 10, 1897, the insurrection was broken, and Aguinaldo with his remaining adherents had taken refuge at Biacnabato, some sixty miles from Manila. He was now without a rival, for Bonifacio had dared to attempt his life, had been brought before a court-martial, had been condemned to death and had disappeared.

Aguinaldo, who now called himself not only Generalissimo of the Army of Liberation but President of the Revolutionary Government, had adopted guerilla warfare, and the Spanish commands were forced to follow an enemy who was never dangerous to large bodies, but who always was to small ones—an enemy who, wearing no uniform, upon the approach of a large body became peaceful labourers in the fields along the road, but were ready to pick up their rifles or bolos and use them against a small party or a straggler. Still, whatever they had fought for at first, the insurgent leaders were now fighting for their own safety.

The governor general sought in various ways to gain the support of the country. He called for Filipino volunteers, and, curiously enough, they responded with enthusiasm. The rapidity with which they were recruited was probably largely due to the activity of the friars. This added to the hatred of them felt by the class of natives represented by Aguinaldo.

Between June and December, 1897, the time was spent in an obscure bargaining, the outcome of which was the so-called Treaty of Biacnabato, which Primo de Rivera—the governor general—has stated was merely a promise to pay a money bribe to the insurgents if they would cease a combat in which they had lost hope of success but which they could still prolong to the detriment of the resources and the prestige of Spain.

The result of the bargainings was that Spain agreed to pay eight hundred thousand Mexican dollars for the surrender of Aguinaldo and his principal leaders and the arms and ammunition in their possession. An amnesty was proclaimed. Aguinaldo and his leaders were sent to Hongkong under escort, where they declared themselves loyal Spanish subjects. Primo de Rivera returned to Spain. As he received in return for the money only about two hundred rifles and a little ammunition, it is not probable that he made any of the promises of changes in the government of the archipelago which the Filipinos have insistently stated since then were the real objects of the agreement.

Whatever may have been the true motives which actuated the Spanish governor general in adopting this method of terminating a successful campaign, he succeeded in purchasing only an armistice and not a peace. On January 23, 1898, a Te Deum was sung in the cathedral of Manila to mark the reëstablishment of peace in the archipelago.

The insurgent leaders had been bought off and their followers had surrendered their arms.

As Spanish dominion in the Philippines was now about to close, let us stop a moment to inquire what it had brought to the Islands. It may have been hard and utterly unprogressive, but it turned the tribes of Luzon and the Visayas from tribal feuds and slave-raiding expeditions to agriculture.

To accomplish these results required untiring energy and a high enthusiasm among the missionaries. They had lived among savages, speaking their tongue, until they had almost forgotten their own. Spain had ceased to be everything to them; their order was their country. Spanish officials came and went, but the ministers of the Church remained, and as they grew to be the interpreters of the wants of the people, in many cases their protectors against spoliation, power fell into their hands. It is rather interesting to learn that in 1619, in the reign of Philip III, it was proposed to abandon the Philippines on account of their useless expense to Spain, but a delegation of friars from the Islands implored him not to abandon the twenty thousand Christians they had converted, and the order was countermanded.

Spanish dominion left the people Christians, whereas, if the Islands had not been occupied by Spain, their people would in all probability to-day be

Mohammedan. The point of view of the Spanish friars may not be ours, but when their efforts are judged by the good rather than the evil results, it can still be said that Spain gave Christianity and a long term of peace to the Philippine archipelago. The Filipinos are the only Christian Asiatics.

But Philippine history was to take an unexpected turn. The Spanish-American war broke out, and a new factor appeared upon the scene in the shape of Commodore Dewey and his fleet. We all know the story of the battle of Manila Bay, but we may just recall it briefly.

It was the night of April 30, 1898, that the American Asiatic squadron, which had received its orders at Hongkong, arrived off the Philippines. They took a look first into Subig Bay, but seeing no enemy, they made their way into Manila Bay by the Boca Grande entrance. There were rumours of mines in the channel and big guns in the forts, but Dewey took the chance, and the fleet steamed in at night. The ships formed two columns, the fighting ships all in one line, and the auxiliary vessels about twelve hundred yards behind. They moved at the rate of their slowest vessel.

Black thunder clouds at times obscured even the crescent moon that partially lighted their course, but occasional lightning flashes gave the bold Americans a glimpse of frowning Corregidor and the sentinel rock of El Fraile. The ships were dark except for one white light at the stern of each as a guide to the vessel next in line. As the *Olympia* turned toward El Fraile her light was seen by a Spanish sentry. A sheet of flame from the smokestack of the *McCulloch*, a revenue cutter attached to the fleet, also betrayed its presence to the enemy at the same moment. El Fraile and a battery on the south shore of the bay at once opened fire, which was returned by the ships to such good purpose that the battery was silenced in three minutes. Slowly, steadily, Dewey's ships steamed on, and at dawn discovered the gray Spanish vessels lying in front of the naval arsenal at Cavite, over on the distant shore to the right. Admiral Montojo's flagship, the *Reina Cristina*, and the *Castilla*, and a number of smaller vessels, formed a curved line of battle, which was protected in a measure by the shore batteries. The Spaniards had one more ship than the Americans, but the latter had bigger guns.

Silently the American squadron advanced across the bay, with the Stars and Stripes flying from every ship. At quarter past five on the morning of May 1st, the Spanish ships fired their first shots. When less than six thousand yards from their line, Dewey gave the famous order to Captain Gridley, in command of the *Olympia*: "You may fire when you're ready, Gridley."

Two hours later, the *Reina Cristina* had been burned, the *Castilla* was on fire, and all but one of the other Spanish vessels were abandoned and sunk. Dewey gave his men time for breakfast and a little rest, then shelled and silenced the batteries at Cavite. Soon after noon the Spaniards surrendered, having lost 381 men and ten war vessels. Seven Americans were slightly wounded, but none were killed. So ended this famous battle.

CHAPTER III
INSURRECTION

Admiral Dewey took a great liking to General Anderson, "Fighting Tom" (L.'s cousin), the first military officer to command the American forces in the Philippines. On one occasion the Admiral fired a salute well after sundown (contrary to naval regulations) to compliment him on his promotion to the rank of major general, and scared the wits out of some of the good people ashore. General Anderson has given me a few notes about his experiences at that time, which are of special interest.

"When in the latter part of April, 1898, I received an order relieving me from duty in Alaska and ordering me to the Philippines, I was engaged in rescuing a lot of people who had been buried by an avalanche in the Chilcoot Pass. I took my regiment at once to San Francisco, and there received an order placing me in command of the first military expedition to the Philippines. This was the first American army that ever crossed an ocean. We were given only two days for preparation. We were not given a wagon, cart, ambulance, or a single army mule, nor boats with which to land our men. I received fifty thousand dollars in silver and was ordered to render what assistance I could. I had never heard of Aguinaldo at that time, and all I knew of the Philippines was that they were famous for hemp, earthquakes, tropical diseases and rebellion.

"We stopped at Honolulu on the way over, although the Hawaiian Islands had not been annexed. The Kanakas received us with enthusiasm and assured us that the place was a paradise before the coming of the missionaries and mosquitoes. From there we went to Guam, where we found nude natives singing 'Lucy Long' and 'Old Dan Tucker,' songs they had learned from American sailors.

"When we reached Cavite the last day of June, Admiral Dewey asked me to go ashore and call on Aguinaldo, who, he assured me, was a native chief of great influence. Our call was to have been entirely informal, but when we approached the house of the Dictator we found a barefooted band in full blare, the bass-drummer after the rule of the country being the leader. The stairway leading to Aguinaldo's apartment was lined on either side by a strange assortment of Filipino warriors. The Chief himself was a small man in a very long-tailed frock coat, and in his hand he held a collapsible opera hat. I saw him many times afterward and always thus provided. He asked me at once if I could recognize his assumption. This I could not do, so when a few days later I invited him to attend our first Fourth of July he declined. He further showed his displeasure by failing to be present at the first dinner to which we American officers were invited. There for the first time we met Filipina ladies. They were bare as to their shoulders, yet in some mysterious way their dresses remained well in place. In dancing there was a continuous shuffling on the floor because their slippers only half covered their light fantastics, rendering them more agile than graceful.

A GROUP OF FILIPINA LADIES.

"In returning from visiting the Tagalog Chief we saw a headless statue of Columbus. I asked a native to explain how Christopher had lost his head. The reply was that they beheaded him because they did not wish to be discovered.

"Soon after I got to Cavite, I was invited with the officers of my staff to attend a dinner given in my honour. At the symposium I was asked to state the principles upon which the American government was founded. I answered, 'The consent of the governed, and majority rule.' Buencamino, the toastmaster, replied, 'We will baptize ourselves to that sentiment,' upon which he emptied his champagne glass on his head. The others likewise wasted their good wine.

"When General Merritt arrived he first came ashore at a village behind the line we had established where Aguinaldo was making his headquarters. Rain was falling in torrents at the time, but Aguinaldo, who must have known of the presence of the new Governor General, failed to ask him to take shelter in his headquarters. Naturally General Merritt was indignant and directed that thereafter any necessary business should be conducted through me. This placed me in a very disagreeable position. At first I thought I could conciliate and use the Filipinos against the Spaniards, but General Merritt brought an order from President McKinley directing that we should only recognize the Filipinos as rebellious subjects of Spain. Aguinaldo reproached me bitterly for my change of conduct toward him, but because of my orders I could not do otherwise, nor could I explain the cause.

"We soon drifted into open hostility. I found but one man who appeared to understand the situation, and he was the much hated Archbishop Nozaleda. After we took Manila he invited me to come to see him. He remarked in the course of our conversation that when we took the city by storm he expected to see our soldiers kill the men and children and violate the women. But instead he praised us for having maintained perfect order. For reply I quoted the Latin, '*Parcere subjectis, et debellare superbos.*' Which prompted him to say in Spanish to a Jesuit priest, 'Why, these people seem to be civilized.' To which the Jesuit replied, 'Yes, we have some colleges in their country.'

"The statement that we seemed to be civilized calls for an explanation. I found many Filipinos feared American rule might prove more severe on them than the Spanish control. In a school book that I glanced at in a Spanish school was the enlightening statement that the Americans were a cruel people who had exterminated the entire Indian population of North America."

The battle of Manila Bay was fought and won, as we well remember, on May Day. Through the kind offices of the British consul the Spanish admiral came to an understanding with Dewey. Surgeons were sent ashore to assist in the care of the wounded Spaniards, and sailors to act as police. The cable was cut, and the blockade was carried into effect at once. The foreign population was allowed to leave for China. German men-of-war kept arriving in the harbour, until there were five in all. It was known that Germany sympathized with Spain, and only the timely arrival of some friendly English ships, and the trenchant diplomacy of our admiral, prevented trouble.

All the rest of that month, and the next, and still the next, the fleet lay at anchor, threatening the city with its guns, but making no effort to take it. The people lived in constant fear of bombardment from the ships which they could so plainly see from the Luneta on their evening promenades. But they could not escape, for Aguinaldo's forces lay encamped behind them in the suburbs. In fact, the refugees were seeking safety within the walls of the city, instead of fleeing from it, for while they had no love for the Spaniards, and were fellow countrymen of the rebel chieftain, they preferred to take their chances of bombardment rather than risk his method of "peaceful occupation."

Of course there was no coöperation between the Americans and the Filipinos, although both wanted the same thing and each played somewhat into the other's hand. Admiral Dewey refused to give Aguinaldo any naval aid, and the *insurrectos* on at least two occasions found it profitable to betray our plans to the common enemy.

The delay in taking the city was caused by Dewey's shortage of troops. He could have taken it at any time, but could not have occupied it. The Spanish commander made little attempt at defense. A formal attack on one of the forts satisfied the demands of honour. When the city surrendered, on August 13th, the Americans were in the difficult position of guarding thirteen thousand Spanish soldiers, of keeping at bay some fourteen thousand plunder-mad Filipinos, and of policing a city of two hundred thousand people—all with some ten thousand men!

The way in which it was accomplished is in effective contrast with European methods. When our troops broke the line of trenches encircling Manila they pressed quickly forward through the residence district to the old walled town, which housed the governmental departments of the city. Here they halted in long lines, resting calmly on their arms until the articles of capitulation were signed. It took but an hour or so to arrange for the disposition of our troops among the various barracks and for the removal of the disarmed Spanish garrison to the designated places of confinement. Then command was passed along by mounted officers for the several regiments to proceed to their quarters for the night. In columns of four they marched off with the easy swing and unconcern of troops on practice march. A thin cordon of sentinels appeared at easy hailing distance along the principal streets, and the task was accomplished.

By noon next day they had a stability as great as though they had been there for years. Not a woman was molested, not a man insulted, and the children on the street were romping with added zest to show off before their new-found friends. The banks felt safe to open their vaults, and the merchants found a healthily rising market. The ships blockaded and idling at anchor in the harbour discharged their cargoes, the customs duties being assessed according to the Spanish tariff by bright young volunteers, aided by interpreters. The streets were cleaned of their accumulated filth, and the courts of law were opened. All this was done under General Anderson's command, and it seems to me is much to his credit.

A daughter of General Anderson's, who was there at the time with her father, writes: "Days of intense anxiety followed the opening of hostilities. The Filipinos were pushed back more and more, but we feared treachery within the city. We heard that they were going to poison our water supply, that they were going to rise and bolo us all, that every servant had his secret instructions. Also, that Manila was to be burned. There proved to be something in this, for twice fires were started and gained some headway, and we women were banished to the transports again."

Aguinaldo had demanded at least joint occupation of the city, and his full share of the loot as a reward for services rendered. We can imagine his disgust at being told that Americans did not loot, and that they intended to hold the city themselves. If there had been no other reason for refusing him, the conduct of his troops in the suburbs would have furnished a sufficient one, for they were utterly beyond control, assaulting and plundering their own brother Filipinos and neutral foreigners, as well as Spaniards, and torturing their prisoners. But this refusal, justifiable as it certainly was, marked the real beginning of the insurrection against American rule, though there was no immediate outbreak.

Aguinaldo was a mestizo school teacher when, in 1896, he became leader of the insurrection against Spain. The money with which Spain hoped to purchase peace was to be paid in three instalments, the principal condition being that the Filipino leaders should leave the Islands. This they did, going to Hongkong, where the first instalment was promptly deposited in a bank. The second instalment, to Aguinaldo's great disgust, was paid over to Filipinos left in the Islands, and the last one was not paid at all. This was just as well for him, because his fellow insurrectionists were already demanding of him an accounting for the funds in Hongkong, and had him summoned to court for the purpose. This proceeding he wisely avoided by leaving for Europe in disguise.

He got only as far as Singapore, however, for there—in April of '98—he heard of the probability of American interference in the Islands and interviewed our consul. The go-between for this interview was an unscrupulous interpreter, whose intrigues were destined to have far-reaching effects for us. It has been charged that both our consul at Singapore and the one at Hongkong committed this nation to a policy favouring Philippine independence, but the whole question of American pledges finally resolves itself into a choice between the word of an American admiral and a Chinese mestizo.

When Spain had failed to pay over to Aguinaldo the balance of the peace money, he had promptly gone to work to organize another revolution from the safe harbourage of Hongkong. His flight to Singapore had interrupted this, but now, with the Americans so conspicuously there to "help," it was a simple matter to put his plans in operation.

A month after the battle of Manila Bay Aguinaldo proclaimed himself "president" (in reality military dictator) of the "Filipino Republic." But this republic existed only on paper. Dewey accurately states the condition of affairs when he says, "Our fleet had destroyed the only government there was, and there was no other government; there was a reign of terror throughout the Philippines, looting, robbing, murdering." A form of municipal election was held, but if a candidate not favoured by the insurgents was elected, he was at once deposed. One candidate won his election by threatening to kill any one who got the office in his place. Persons "contrary minded" were not allowed to vote. These happenings hardly suggest a republican form of government, but they are typical of conditions at that time.

AGUINALDO'S PALACE AT MALOLOS.

Naturally the self-styled president was not recognized by the American officials, and they were justified, as is shown by the fact that before the year was up Aguinaldo himself had come to realize that he could not maintain order among his people, and tried to resign from his office.

Meanwhile his lack of recognition by the Americans, and his exclusion from the spoils of war, so far as Manila was concerned, showed him that his only hope of achieving his ambitions lay in driving these interlopers from the Islands. But for the time being, while awaiting a propitious moment for attack, he occupied himself and his men by conquering the Spaniards in the outlying provinces. Since there was no coöperation among the Spanish forces, he was quite successful. Having proclaimed the republic with himself at the head, he felt justified in maintaining, with the aid of his booty, a truly regal state in his palace at Malolos, aping the forms and ceremonies of the Spanish governors in Manila.

As fast as Church property, or property belonging to Spaniards, fell into his hands, it was confiscated and turned over to the State—if Aguinaldo can be considered the State. His houses and those of his generals were furnished from Spanish possessions, all title deeds were systematically destroyed or hidden, and administrators were appointed for the property.

At the beginning of the new year (1899), he turned his attention to the Americans, and Manila. Because our forces seemed reluctant to fight, the

Filipinos, like the Mexicans to-day, believed that they must be cowards and afraid to meet them. A Mexican paper has recently told its readers what a simple matter it would be, if war were declared, for their troops to cross the border and crush such slight opposition as may be offered to the capture of Washington. So it is no wonder that the Filipinos felt confident of success, especially after their victories over the Spaniards in the outlying regions.

By January, Admiral Dewey, General Anderson and General Merritt had left the Philippine Islands and General Otis was in command. He announced that the government of the United States would be extended over the islands of the archipelago. Next day Aguinaldo retorted with what was virtually a declaration of war. From then on he and his advisers hastened their preparations for the conflict. Members of the native militia who were living in Manila under the protection of the American garrison were warned to stand ready to receive the signal which should start the sack and pillage of the city and the massacre of its inhabitants. By the end of January there were about thirty thousand Filipinos under arms fronting the American lines outside the city, all keyed up for the moment when they should be let loose to drive the Americans into the sea. This time the spoils of Manila should not be snatched from them!

The signal for the advance was to be a conflagration in Manila. Ten thousand militiamen were to rise, set fire to the city, free the Spanish prisoners of war, arm them with arms stored in the arsenal, and attack the Americans. They were to be promptly aided in this last detail by the thirty thousand Filipinos waiting outside, who, surrounding the city, would drive back the fourteen thousand American soldiers upon their burning citadel and upon the two hundred thousand Filipinos, who would by this time have joined their countrymen. If everything had worked out as he had planned, Aguinaldo might very probably have entered the city.

He chose a night early in February, at a time when he knew the American reinforcements which had been ordered could not yet have arrived. Firing began about nine o'clock in the evening, near the San Juan bridge, and continued during the night. Meanwhile, the militia in the city tried to assemble, but the groups were promptly fired on and dispersed. In the morning the ships of Dewey's fleet opened fire from the flanks of the American line. A little later our troops sprang forward and swept their antagonists before their fierce attack. In this encounter the Filipinos lost about eight hundred, and the Americans two hundred and fifty.

For a week the insurgents were quite demoralized, and no wonder, for this was not the way they had expected the "cowardly" Americans to act. But when they saw that our men did not follow up their advantage by pursuit, their courage revived and they began once more to believe those things which they wished to believe. Our troops had to stay where they were because they had not sufficient transportation to take them anywhere else, because the enemy within the city still needed their attention, and because their reinforcements had not arrived.

SAN JUAN BRIDGE.

When these came, General Otis divided his forces. General MacArthur began a movement from his right against the insurgents, who contested every village and locality capable of defense, and burned every train before abandoning it to American hands. The insurgent capital, Malolos, was occupied. In April, General Lawton took Santa Cruz. The American casualties during these operations were about ten thousand officers and men, but the sick report listed fifteen per cent of the expedition, mostly from heat prostration.

General Lawton, who went out early in 1899, and was killed in December of the same year at San Mateo, is believed to have been perhaps the most able of our commanders.

Uniformly the Filipinos lost, but when their courage waned their officers would announce that they had won a big victory somewhere else. In one day, they reported, we had lost twenty-eight thousand men, in a region where in the entire month we had lost but fifty-six. On another occasion they announced that two thousand colonels had been killed. They must have thought our troops were all from Kentucky.

All summer and into the fall this more or less formal and regular warfare continued. But by that time Aguinaldo had decided that while a concentrated field army might appear more impressive to foreigners and be better for advertising purposes, it was not effective for his purpose, and some change must be made. The discontent among the conservative men who still had anything to lose was increasing, while the labourers in the fields, the fishermen, and the great masses of the people were growing weary of the war and the exactions of the commanders of their troops. The spell which Aguinaldo had cast over Luzon was almost broken. The war was nearly over, it seemed—in a civilized country it would have been over.

GENERAL LAWTON.

To the Americans it appeared that the insurrection had been destroyed, and that all they now had to do was to sweep up the remnants of the insurgent forces by a system of police administration not likely to be either difficult or dangerous. In November, MacArthur had his force ready to strike anything within reach, but there seemed to be nothing within reach to strike. He soon came to the conclusion that there was no organized resistance left, that the insurgent army had broken into fragments which would soon become banditti. The disbandment of the insurgent field forces, which the American authorities took to mean the coming of a general submission to our rule, was followed by a long period of inactivity. This, of course, strengthened the impression, but the time was being used by the Filipinos to prepare for a new method of warfare and to organize for resistance by means of a general banding of the people together in support of the guerillas in the field.

To obtain this necessary coöperation the leaders announced the inflexible principle that every native residing within the limits of the archipelago owed active individual allegiance to the insurgent cause. This was enforced by severe penalties, including burial alive, which were systematically exacted. There was little resistance on the part of the victims, who accepted the new policy with a curious combination of loyalty, apathy, ignorance and timidity.

In this way there arose a strange system of dual government, in many cases the town officials openly serving the Americans while they were secretly aiding the insurrection, and with apparently equal solicitude for both. Each town was the base for the neighbouring guerillas, and when a band was too hard pressed it would dissolve and take refuge in its own community. This was easy enough to accomplish, with the aid of the people, for it took very little to transform a Filipino soldier into a good imitation of a peaceful native.

Several months before the formal declaration of guerilla warfare in November of 1899, the Filipino commanders had adopted a policy of occupying a succession of strong defensive positions and forcing our army to a never ending repetition of tactical deployments. This they did with such skill that they were for a time successful. The native force would hover within easy distance of the American camps, but would avoid close conflict and temporarily disband. This would not be regarded by them as a calamity, but simply as a change from one form of action to another, and even a positive advantage.

By February of 1900, General Bates had succeeded in scattering the larger bodies in the south of Luzon, and while some of the Filipino leaders and their followers abandoned the cause, which they saw was hopeless, others returned to the life of bandits, which in many cases had probably been their profession before the war. When their guns were gone they took up the knife and the torch. They did not cease to call themselves soldiers of the republic, but they were not in reality.

By September General MacArthur, who had succeeded General Otis in command of the American forces in the Islands, realized that the opposition to American control came from the towns, and that the guerilla bands could not exist without their support. At first he thought that on account of the efficiency of his troops, the natives would be actuated both by conviction and self-interest to support him. But four months later he saw that further pressure was needed to secure this. So he ordered that all persons suspected of contraband traffic with insurgent organizations should be arrested and sent to Manila. In January, 1901, he ordered the deportation to Guam of twenty-six Filipino leaders, sympathizers, and agents, who were to remain there until peace had been formally declared. Two months later, Aguinaldo was captured by the dare-devil Funston of "the Suicide Squad."

The effect of this measure was to alarm the leaders, of course, who now realized that they could be held responsible for their acts. Orders were also issued that all men who surrendered should be disarmed but released at once, while those captured in the field or arrested in the towns should be held in custody till the end of the war. A letter was found, written by a bandit leader, in March, saying that he was ordered to "proceed more rapidly" with his operations, "as Bryan ordered Emilio (Aguinaldo) to keep the war going vigorously until April." However true that may have been, it is certain that the encouragement which the insurgents received from the country they were fighting much prolonged hostilities and caused the loss of many lives on both sides.

It is hard to realize at this distance the lengths to which the anti-imperialists went, or were willing to go, in those days. Governor Pack told me of an experience he had with one of them—a New Englander of good family and American antecedents. Pack was on his way out to the Islands at the time, and on arriving at Hongkong received the tidings of McKinley's assassination. He was surprised to see this man, a fellow-passenger, rush up to a Filipino with the news and shake his hand, congratulating him on what had happened. The Governor, then a young civilian, could not forget the shocking incident and later, when they shared the same stateroom on the small boat for Manila, he discovered papers which proved that his companion intended to furnish aid and encouragement to any natives who wished to fight against American "tyranny." This discovery gave Pack his appointment as one of the seven lieutenant governors of the hill tribes. But the other man was punished only by being refused entrance to the Islands. It was the stupid and foolish fashion in America then—as indeed it still is—to call this particular form of treason Idealism, and be lenient with it.

Our soldiers found it difficult to take seriously the bands of half naked men, who, they knew, had been pillaging the villages of their own race. It was true that these bands were difficult to pursue and capture, but an army which fought only from ambush, whose detachments fell only upon stragglers and carefully avoided the main body of its enemy, and which showed no regard for the sacredness of a flag of truce, could not inspire much respect. Plunder appeared to be the sole excuse for its existence, and the pompous titles assumed by its commanders were amusing for the leaders of robbers. The Americans followed the retreating bandits without hatred and without fear. But they became weary of the eternal pursuit, and felt a growing irritation.

The Filipinos, however, felt very differently about their soldiers, and it is only fair to give their side too, especially as it may throw some light on the Mexican situation. Even the richest and most highly educated men found nothing to laugh at in these poor bands which were after all composed of their own people fighting and suffering for a cause which they could at least understand, whether or not they sympathized with it. They did not regard the pillaging, tortures, and murders to which the Filipinos subjected their own people as we did. They called the robbery "collecting contributions for the support of the war." As for the murders—in the Orient to kill is an immemorial right of the rulers of men. What if they did fight disguised as peaceful country folk? They were a weak people fighting against a strong. They were naked and they were hungry, and they were fighting for a cause. Their arms were often of little use, and they made powder out of match heads and cartridge shells out of the zinc roofs of parish buildings, and even then they had only ammunition enough to fire a few volleys and then run. But men so armed had forced the United States to send out nearly seventy thousand well equipped soldiers to subdue them. To the native Filipino, as perhaps to the Mexican to-day, the ragged and half savage figures of the guerillas stood for their vision of a united race.

But it was natural that our troops could not understand this, and that they should gradually become embittered against their antagonists. The officers, by the necessary division of our forces, found themselves confronted with conditions utterly alien to their experience. They had to live in native houses or churches, in the midst of four or five thousand people whose language they did not speak, and whose thoughts were not their thoughts. Most of them were young men. They came from all over the United States, and were neither monsters nor saints, but good examples of their time and country.

When these officers learned that the dignified Asiatics who called upon them daily, who drank with them, who talked with them, and who held offices under our government, were also spies of the guerila leaders, secretly aiding those who were anxious to win the price set on their heads, they were hardly pleased. When they found that every movement of the guerillas was reported to them just too late to be of any use, while every movement of their own small forces was promptly made known to the enemy, and when they were present at the disinterment of the twisted bodies of the men who had been buried alive because they were loyal to us, they decided that stricter measures were necessary. This was a state of war. Within wide limits their will was law. Upon their judgment hung not merely their lives and those of their men, but the honour of their country and their regiment. Perhaps in some cases they met cruelty with cruelty, but they at least tried to be honest and just. And the people came to realize this, and also that they were not afraid, with the result that whole communities transferred their allegiance from their own guerila leaders to a single young American, not because he understood them or sympathized with them, but because he was a man whom they could trust and respect.

It was July of 1902, four years after our taking of Manila, before the Islands could be officially declared pacified. Let us hope that the lessons which we learned then may not be forgotten in our dealings with Mexico.[14]

CHAPTER IV
FOLLOWING THE FLAG

They taught Filipinos the right way to work,
And they taught as if teaching were fun;
They taught them to spell and to build themselves roads,
And the best way to handle a gun.
Were their salaries so big that the task was worth while?
Did they save a centavo of pay?
Have the average men an account with the bank?
Never a cent—not they.

So we haven't a job and we haven't a cent,
And nobody cares a damn;
But we've done our work and we've done it well,
To the glory of Uncle Sam,
And we've seen a lot, and we've lived a lot
In these islands over the sea—
Would we change with our brothers grown rich at home?
Praise be to God—not we.

From "The Swan Song," in the Manila Bulletin.

It is, strangely enough, to the influence of that arch anti-imperialist, William Jennings Bryan, that we owe the ratification of the Treaty of Paris, which not only ended the war with Spain but expressly provided for the purchase of the Philippine Islands. The Democrats were opposed to the treaty and were powerful enough in the Senate to have held it up, had not Bryan used his authority to secure the two-thirds vote needed for its ratification. It is amusing to note that a year later, after enabling us to acquire the islands, he used all his power to prevent our keeping them. He was at this time in need of a popular plank in his third presidential platform, and the sorrows of the Filipinos suited his purpose admirably.

Soon after the Treaty of Paris, and long before the end of the insurrection, McKinley appointed a commission of experts to go out to the Islands and report to him on conditions there. They found a country whose civilization was, to put it hopefully, at a standstill. It was too big a problem to be straightened out by a few ambitious Filipinos. The Commission returned to America convinced of the necessity of our occupation.

Congress soon passed a special organic act for the organization of a civil government in the Islands, to succeed the military rule then in force. In 1900, President McKinley appointed the second Commission, headed by Mr. Taft, which was instructed to assume control of the Islands, gradually relieving the army wherever conditions allowed of their doing so.

This Commission had five members, three of them lawyers (two of whom had been on the bench), and two professors. Its functions were at first legislative and judicial, but in 1901, when the president of the Commission, Mr. Taft, became Governor General of the Islands, the other members were given the portfolios of the different departments and executive power in the pacified parts of the Islands. Dean C. Worcester, a member of the earlier Commission and already an authority on the Philippines, became the first Minister of the Interior; Luke E. Wright, the Vice Governor, had the Department of Commerce and Police; H. C. Ide, former Chief Justice of Samoa, had charge of Finance and Justice, while Professor Moses was put at the head of Public Instruction. Governor Taft became really the "Father of the Philippines," for when he left the Islands in 1904 to become Secretary of War he had even higher authority over them than he had had as governor, while still later, as President of the United States, he was able to see that the same high standard of appointments was maintained.[15]

McKinley charged this Commission that their work was "*not to subjugate, but to emancipate.*" We made many mistakes, for we were new to the business and dealing with a strange people, but until very lately even the selfishness which is supposed to be inherent in party politics has been absent in our dealings with this people, whom we considered our sacred charge. No one ever asked an American official in the Islands what his politics were. Even the governorship itself was out of the reach of the spoilsman. Of the five governors who were appointed by the Republican administrations, only one besides the first governor belonged to the dominant party, and he was in office but a few months.

Since the Taft Commission first organized, several changes have taken place. Filipino members have been added, and it has acquired the character of an upper house, rather than a legislature. The work of a lower house is done by the Assembly, made up of eighty-one members chosen by the people of the Christian tribes. They have no authority over the Moro and other non-Christian tribes, which are legislated for by the Commission directly. To-day the Filipinos control their municipal and county governments, but their finances are kept under supervision.

The problems which the Commissioners had to solve were many and varied. Trade was at a standstill. During the last normal year under Spain the exports from the Islands had amounted to about sixteen million dollars. By 1912 they had more than trebled. There was also a currency problem. Coins from everywhere—Mexico, China, America, India—were in common circulation, with almost daily fluctuations in value. The Islands now have their own money on a gold basis. Then, close on the heels of the insurrection, came a famine. Locusts swept over the land and destroyed what little grain the war had left. The natives in some parts of the archipelago ate the locusts, however, and liked them, making the work of the officials more difficult. Grain shipped from America decayed in the storehouses before it could be distributed, and, as if that were not enough, carabaos died by the thousand from rinderpest.

But the most difficult of all was the problem of the friar lands. Thousands of acres of valuable land had been acquired during Spanish rule by the different orders of monks, and held by them with great profit. One of the chief causes of Aguinaldo's rebellion was the exactions of these wealthy churchmen, which galled a patient people into final revolt, and during the ascendancy of the insurgent government resulted in the confiscation of Church property and the flight of the friars. These men took refuge in Manila, and petitioned the new government for a settlement of their claims. Their legal rights were not to be disputed, but to return them to their property and protect them there would have brought on us the increased enmity of a people whose friendship we were trying to win. The friends of the friars were no friends of the people. It was decided to have the Philippine Government buy these lands from the Church, which was accordingly arranged. Even this was not a popular solution, but seems to have been the best that could be done under the circumstances. One-third of these lands are still vacant.

Road building was one of the most baffling of the problems. The people had no appreciation of the necessity for good roads, and would not pay for them nor help keep them in repair when they were built. For years the Commission toiled at the seemingly hopeless task, and it was not until Governor Forbes went out there from Boston that anything definite was accomplished. His native city should be very proud of his brilliantly successful administration, the proofs of which met us at every turn during our stay in the archipelago, and convinced us of the fatal mistake it is to allow such a position as Governor of the Philippines to become the prize of politicians. To the native mind his name became inseparably connected with roads. *Caminero* means a road man, and Cameron Forbes is of course known to the Filipino as "Caminero Forbays." He had been a commissioner five years when made governor general, which office he held for four more. When Mr. Wilson became president, Governor Forbes was advised not to tender his resignation, for it was believed the new administration would wish to keep the Islands clear of the spoil system.

BENGUET ROAD

Suddenly out of a clear sky, the Governor General received this cablegram from the Insular Bureau:

"Harrison confirmed August 21st. The President desires him to sail September 10th. Will it be convenient to have your resignation accepted September 1st. Harrison to accept and take the oath of office September 2nd. The President desires to meet your convenience. Should Harrison take linen, silver, glass, china and automobiles? What else would you suggest? Wife and children will accompany him. Please engage for him servants you leave."

Worst of all, it was given out to the papers before the Governor received it, so that certain anti-American sheets in Manila had the pleasure of flaunting the news on their front pages for him to read. Surely some more considerate and courteous method of retiring a fine administrator might have been devised than this abrupt and rude dismissal, and it would seem that petty household matters might have been kept separate.

Secretary Worcester, also a native of New England, who is the greatest living authority on the Islands, and whose achievements with the wild, non-Christian tribes had been marvelous—to say nothing of his other excellent work—had also of course to resign. Forbes, by the way, is not a Republican, but neither is he a Democrat, and Independents are not politically useful.

The work of the administration immediately preceding that of Governor Harrison is worth at least a partial summary. Besides building roads, establishing a good health resort at Baguio, systematizing the work of the government, reducing the number of bureaus, cutting down expenses and eliminating duplication of work, and numerous other public services, Governor Forbes succeeded in accomplishing the following:

The reorganization of the merchant marine.

The construction of aids to navigation—buoys, lighthouses and beacons, wharves and harbours.

The removal of restrictions from shipping.

The establishment of a policy for the exclusive use of permanent materials in construction, practically all the construction in the Islands being done of reinforced concrete and selected woods.

The passage of a law providing for proper development of irrigation, laying aside an annual sum for that purpose.

The establishment of a cadastral law for registering law titles. "Under this system it was possible to get land titles settled, one of the most difficult and important problems confronting any government and one bearing directly on the welfare of the people in various ways.

"A general system was adopted of loaning to provinces and municipalities to encourage them in the construction of public works, particularly those of a revenue-bearing nature; most especially markets, which improved the sanitary condition of the food supply and proved both popular with the people and profitable for the municipalities; these markets usually paid for themselves in five years from the increased revenues.

FIRST PHILIPPINE ASSEMBLY.

"The Governor's influence was used throughout to make the instruction in the schools practical in its nature; children were taught to make things that would prove to be salable and which would give them a living. The dignity of labour was emphasized. Encouragement was given to foster the construction of railroads.

"The establishment of a postal savings bank encouraged the children to invest. Prizes were given for that child or school which showed the best record." (Governor Forbes took an especial interest in the latter.)

The first general election was held in the Islands on the third of July, 1907, to choose delegates for the Assembly. Before that the Philippine Commission had been the sole legislative body. The delegates were chosen from the thirty-five Christian provinces. At that time only a minute percentage of the population, even among the Filipinos, was qualified to meet the simple conditions which would enable them to vote, and to-day the percentage is far from large. The electorate consists mainly of two classes, the ilustrados, or educated natives and mestizos,[16] and the *taos*, or peasants. The latter are not only ignorant but indifferent, with no vision beyond what their eyes can see, and no interest in who governs them, so long as crops are good and taxes low. One of the tasks of our representatives is to educate and awaken these people to responsible citizenship. It is a task still far from accomplishment.

It must be admitted that the work of the Assembly to-day, after eight years of fair trial, does not encourage Filipinization of the service. It is fortunate—at times—that the two legislative bodies have equal power not only to initiate legislation but to block the passage of each other's bills. In this way the Commission has been able to hold up some of the freak legislation sent up to it by the lower body. The Manila *Times* has published a list of the laws which were wanted by the Filipino assemblymen recently. They spent the valuable time of the entire first session talking them over and the Commission refused to concur. One was to increase their own salaries, of course. Another was to erect monuments to all the ilustrados who had cried "*Bajo los Americanos*" most loudly. Others wanted to fly the Philippine flag above the American on all masts, to make a legal holiday of the birthday of Rizal's grandmother, and to free all prisoners, no matter what their crimes.

OSMEÑA, THE SPEAKER OF THE FIRST ASSEMBLY.

As may be imagined, a body of men which can pass such bills is quite capable of blocking the sane legislation which comes to them for approval, and unfortunately they have the power to do this. The way in which the slavery question was handled illustrates their methods.

Slavery was known to exist in the Islands, and to take two forms,—actual slavery, where one person was sold by another, and a sort of semi-slavery, or peonage, where a man sold his services for debt.

The peon was given his keep, but the interest on his debt was added faster than he could earn. He was really a slave, except that he had sold himself rather than been sold by another. But his debts might be bought and sold, so that it amounted to the same thing in the end. Interest was sometimes as high as ten per cent a month, while fifty cents a month was allowed for his services. Worcester in his book tells of a man who borrowed $1.25, which he and his wife and children worked several years in the effort to repay; but by that time the amount had become $37.50!

Spain had nominally abolished slavery long before, but it had continued in force in both the Christian and non-Christian provinces. The legislators themselves held peons. The law of Congress creating the Philippine Government prohibited slavery, but there are no penalties attached, so it could not be enforced.

The Filipinos denied that slavery existed in the Islands. Worcester made a careful investigation, and an exhaustive report on both slavery and peonage. All but a few copies of this report were burned by a Filipino official. It was a subject which neither the Filipino politician nor their self-styled friends the anti-imperialists wished to see discussed in print. The Manila papers had been absolutely silent on the subject, and even the anti-slavery legislation which was finally forced through, after having been tabled again and again without so much as the briefest formality of discussion, passed unnoticed. It was a sore subject, and the Filipino method of treating a sore subject is not to heal it, but to refrain from discussing it.

There is no question but we have given the Filipinos too much power for their own good. They now, under the Democratic Administration, have five members in the Commission, to America's four. They have to-day much power—only colonies such as Canada and Australia have more, while Egypt has been given less in a generation than the Filipinos have received in ten years.

The present governor, Francis Burton Harrison, has been severely criticized. His party was pledged to a rapid Filipinization which has proved disastrous, for it was devised by men wholly ignorant of the situation. The destruction of the wonderful civil service system so carefully built up in the early days as an object lesson to Spanish-bred politicians, is only one of many changes which have been brought about.

We have certainly lost prestige in the Islands under the Democratic Administration. Filipinos no longer remove their hats during the playing of the Star Spangled Banner on the Luneta, so Governor Harrison finally tried to discontinue the playing of the national anthem. The American community would not stand this, however, so it was resumed. In many other ways the Filipinos have become "cocky." This of course does not apply to the tao, who plods along regardless of politics.

A friend wrote me recently, "I don't think I could give you a more accurate idea of what most Americans and British, and even intelligent natives, think of this Democratic administration than to repeat a conversation I overheard in the Fort McKinley cars one morning between two coloured American soldiers. They began by laughing at Harrison's 'give them what they want' speech, and speaking of the Filipinos as 'spoiled children.' 'Well,' said one dusky brave, 'we have one more year of this rotten administration, then, thank Gawd, we'll have a white man's government!'"

Professor Thomas Lindsey Blayney writes in one of the magazines: "I talked with business men, native and foreign educators, clergymen, army and navy officers, editors American and British, and many Filipinos of undoubted patriotism and intelligence, and I do not hesitate to assure you that the demoralizing tendency of the policies of the present American administration in the Islands is deserving of the widest publicity." The situation, he says, "is bidding fair to become a national disgrace if we allow politics and sentiment to take the place of reason and justice." He goes on to say, "There is no phenomenon of our national life more passing strange than that which induces many of our good people to accept the statements of paid emissaries of the Filipino junto, or some of our new and inexperienced officials at Manila, rather than those of our fellow countrymen of long administrative experience in the Islands.... The loss of men like Governor Forbes, Mr. Worcester, Dr. Heiser, and others, is looked upon as a distinct setback in the development of better and more stable institutions in the entire Orient in the interest of humanity as a whole."

All of which only bears out what Lord Cromer told Mr. Forbes—"If your personnel employed in the administration of dependencies at a distance becomes subject to change with changing political parties, you are doomed to failure in your effort to govern countries overseas."

There has recently been a great financial depression in the Islands, due partly to hoarding against threatened independence, and partly to the difficulty the new Filipino officials of the Bureau of Internal Revenue find in collecting the usual amount. A slump in real estate followed quickly upon the news that we might shortly leave the Islands. Rinderpest, the cattle plague which had worked such havoc and which had finally been conquered after tremendous expenditure of money and energy, broke out again immediately upon the substitution of Filipinos for white men in the service. Some time the good people at home will learn that giving a child candy because it cries for candy is not always the best thing for the child. The Filipinos are in many ways children, delightful ones, with charming manners, but needing a firm and even rule till they come of age and take over their own affairs. Most Filipinos of intelligence realize this. In fact, they have of late been rushing in petitions signed by their best and most influential citizens urging the retention of the Islands in their present standing.

What the Filipino wishes for himself depends upon the man. Only one in ten, among the civilized tribes, knows anything about the discussion of independence. The taos would like independence if they believe it to be what their politicians have told them—freedom to do as they please, and exemption from taxes. Otherwise they are not interested.

When the Jones bill was being discussed a Moro elevator boy at the War Department in Washington was asked, "If the Filipinos are given their independence, how will you feel?" "I am an American now," he answered, "but if that happen—I go back, and with the Moros fight the Filipinos!"

Most people fail to realize that the Islands are no financial burden to this country. They are, and have always been, wholly self-supporting. Their revenues pay their bills, and their taxes, incidentally, are the lowest in the civilized world. We keep soldiers there but only the cost of their transportation is extra.

Our rule in the Philippines has been the greatest of all paradoxes, a benevolent despotism working ardently for its own destruction. This is very unusual, and rather fine. We ought to be proud of what we have done, and very anxious to see the work well finished. Good men have given their lives for it, and few of those who lived have come out after years of thankless toil in a tropical land, with as much as they had when they went into the service. We owe it to them and to our helpless wards, as well as to our national honour, to see the thing through.

CHAPTER V
HEALING A NATION

The sanitary conditions which existed in the Islands twenty odd years ago would seem to us appalling, but perhaps they were no worse than those of some other tropical countries at that time. Even the most progressive colonizers, like the English, had given up trying radical reforms, contenting themselves with making passably healthful conditions, especially for the European part of the towns. The combination of climate and native inertia seemed to them one which it was difficult and almost hopeless to combat. So it remained for us to prove that the thing could be done—that a tropical country could be made sanitary and hygienic for all its inhabitants, whether they were white or brown or yellow, and whether they wanted it made so or not. If we had done nothing else for our restless dependency, that achievement would be a sufficient crown of glory.

Manila was then, as it still is, the most highly civilized spot in the Islands. As I have said, much of the walled city was built of stone and plaster, but many of the natives in the suburbs lived in one-room houses made of wood and raised on stilts. No provision whatever was made for drainage or for the removal of garbage. Each house was a law unto itself and very often an offense unto its neighbours.

A Carabao

A large part of the city drained, directly or indirectly, into the Pasig River. Here, also, the carabao, which is not a fastidious animal, went for his mud baths, and the women washed their clothes. This river furnished drinking water for all who lived near enough to share the privilege. It was said to have a flavour like the Ganges, which they sorely missed later on when a purer supply was substituted.

The medieval wall, which allowed for many damp, unhealthy corners, interfered with municipal ventilation. No cleansing winds can sweep through a city whose every street ends in a high wall. Outside was a stagnant moat which made a convenient breeding place for the industrious mosquito.

The local market used to be a community dwelling for all the vendors, who lived there, reveling in their filth. Their children were born there, also their dogs, pigs, cats, and chickens. It was so vile smelling that no American dared go into it. Never being cleaned, it was the center from which disease was spread to the city.

These markets were the first places to be cleaned by the Americans. The first step was always to burn up the entire shed, and then build an iron and concrete structure, which could be washed down every night with a hose. Only the night watchman was allowed to live there.

This is only typical of changes made in every department, from market to school, from custom house to palace. To tell a long story very shortly, gaps have been opened in the city walls to let in the air, the moat has been filled in with soil dredged from the bay to make a field for sports, nearby marshes have been reclaimed and old wells filled up, while a sewerage system and a method of collecting refuse have of course been established. The new water system has cut the death rate from water-borne diseases in half. To stop an epidemic whole districts of huts which could not be fumigated were burned and others were sprayed with strong disinfectants by fire engines. Slowly the people are being taught the rules of hygiene. The new and up-to-date medical school is turning out very good doctors, and the school of nursing, most excellent nurses, who are gentle, cheerful and dainty.

The modern hospitals were at first regarded with suspicion by the natives, who went with the greatest reluctance for treatment. But to-day the difficulty is to keep them out. A toothache is excuse enough for a week's sojourn with free board. The native doctor often is a skilful grafter, and has to be watched, otherwise he may pass in all his poor relations, more to give them food and rest than for illness. A friend was much annoyed while sick in a Manila hospital by some Filipina girls in pink and lilac hospital gowns who were romping through the corridors. Her nurse explained that they were passed in by the native doctor. One of these physicians had every bed in his ward filled with patients who were not ill but just enjoying themselves. Some of these doctors abuse their authority in other ways. One of them, it was discovered, used to go to San Lazaro, the hospital for contagious diseases, and take friends who were detained there with leprosy to ride in public vehicles.

But aside from occasional abuses by natives, the work which has been done for the public health in Manila is an example of what has been accomplished elsewhere. In many of the provincial towns the introduction of artesian wells has brought the death rate tumbling down to half its former size. The work was carried on under disadvantages at first, for it was the butt of much ridicule and abuse—the former from abroad, the latter from the native press. Medical authorities in other parts of the Far East laughed at our efforts to create better conditions for the Filipinos, and told us that Orientals were incapable of sanitary reforms. Before long, these same men were seeking to learn by what magic we had accomplished what they had hardly dared even attempt, and were sending delegates to Manila to study our methods.[17]

When Americans went there they found the Filipinos a race of semi-invalids. Those who had managed to survive the various scourges which were constantly sweeping the Islands were often infected with hookworm or similar parasites which sapped their vitality. Many of them were tubercular, and most of them were under-fed. The laziness which made several Filipino workmen equal to one American was much of it due to actual physical weakness. As a people, they are showing a marked improvement in energy and activity. It was from changes of this sort that the would-be benevolent anti-imperialists laboured to save them.

Of course, a great deal remains for us to do. Half the babies still die before they are a year old. Only a beginning has been made in stamping out tuberculosis. The people have not yet been educated out of that fatalism which makes them prefer acceptance of evil to fighting it. But as fast as they learn English they come under our educative influence more and more.

Dr. Richard P. Strong, whom we knew when we were in the Islands and who is now at the Harvard Medical School lecturing on tropical diseases, has done many notable things in various parts of the world. We all know about his wonderful work in the northern part of China, when the pneumonic plague[18] was raging there a few years ago, and still later his heroism among the typhus-stricken soldiers of Serbia. But we do not all know that, among other things, he has discovered a cure for a dreadful skin disease called yaws, which has been prevalent in the Philippines. A doctor in Bontoc cured a case with a single injection of salvarsan. The "case" was so delighted that he escaped from the hospital before a second injection could be given him, rushed home to his native village, and returned a day or so later with a dozen or more of his neighbours who were suffering from the same trouble.

We were fortunate in traveling through the Islands with Dr. Heiser, who had entire control of the health conditions there for many years—in fact, until the Democratic administration. To him is largely due the practical disappearance of smallpox from the Philippines. When the Americans took over the country there were sometimes over fifty thousand deaths a year from this one disease. The change is the direct result of the ten million vaccinations which were performed by American officials. An effort was made to entrust the vaccinating to Filipino officials, but epidemics kept breaking out, and it was discovered that their work was being done chiefly on paper.

In a recent letter a friend writes, "The other day one of our servants, Crispin, was ill. I tried to get him to go to the hospital, but he insisted he was not sick. I did not enjoy having him wait on the table, for I thought he had measles. So I took him to the hospital myself and told him to do what the doctor said. When I returned home a telephone call summoned us to the hospital to be vaccinated at once, for Crispin had the smallpox! They sent him to San Lazaro, where he had a good time, and came home smiling, while we spent a miserable ten days waiting to see what was going to happen to us. The native *saindados* came promptly to disinfect, but all they did was to put a bucket of something in the center of the room. I soon saw that they were not going to be thorough, so after ten minutes, just as they were going away, I called them back and telephoned to the board of health, asking if no American sanitary officer was coming. They said no, that Filipinos had been put in all the white men's places. So I went to work myself, burning bedding, clothes and hangings, and opening every trunk and closet. It was a revelation to those two little natives, who thought they had done enough before."

Apparently the natives had the same aversion to the preventive method of vaccination that some of our own countryfolk have, for Dr. Heiser writes of the early work in the field: "Formerly ... the lives of the vaccinators were seriously threatened by persons who refused to be vaccinated. However, after much persuasion, a considerable number of the inhabitants were vaccinated. Shortly afterwards smallpox was introduced and the death rate among the unvaccinated became alarming; the people themselves then noted that in spite of the fact that the vaccinated persons frequently came in constant contact with the disease they did not contract it, while the unvaccinated died in large numbers. This led to urgent request being made for vaccination and the vaccinators who previously found their lives in constant danger were welcomed."

But perhaps Dr. Heiser's greatest work has been done in freeing the Islands of the worst-feared disease of all times and nations—leprosy. I was walking along the street with him one day when he noticed the swollen ear lobes of a man near by. It was one of the first symptoms of leprosy. He stopped and spoke to the man and walked with him to the hospital. The disease is not really so much to be feared as people think, for it is seldom inherited and is not easily contagious.

We had planned to go to Culion, the beautiful island where thousands of lepers have been taken to live or to die, and where they have every care and comfort that science and unselfish devotion can give them. Unfortunately for us, the Secretary of War was obliged to cut the trip short, owing to official business in Manila, so we did not go there. We heard so much about the place that this was a real disappointment.

The island is a day's sail from Manila. It is well forested, and has hills and fertile valleys and a fine harbour. The more important buildings of the town which the authorities knew would be needed by the thousands of lepers then at large, were built from the foundations entirely of concrete, for sanitary reasons and economy. Besides hundreds of houses, one finds there to-day a theater, a town hall, a school, dining halls, hospitals, stores, docks and warehouses. Water, lighting and sewerage systems were also constructed, and a separate settlement was built for the non-leprous employees.

Culion is really a leper's heaven. The people have perfect freedom, and live normal lives, farming or fishing when they are able, carrying on their own government, having their own police force, playing in the band if they are musical, giving theatrical performances. They have social distinctions, too—those better born take the place denied them in the outer world because of their affliction. Here they are again Somebody.

When Americans took possession of the Islands there were six thousand lepers at large. Two things evidently had to be done—first, prevent a further spread of the disease; and second, cure those who already had it, if this were possible.

Segregation of all known cases, as fast as accommodations could be provided for them, was the immediate necessity. The colony at Culion was opened in 1906 with five hundred patients. These went reluctantly to their new abode, but once settled there, found it so much to their liking that they wrote home enthusiastically, and after that the authorities had no difficulty in persuading others to go. Indeed, the plight of these poor outcasts had been pitiful enough. They were so neglected that in one of the larger cities they had been known to go into the markets and handle the produce, as a protest against their treatment.

More than eight thousand have been transferred to Culion in all, and to-day every known leper in the Philippines is there. New cases are still occasionally found, but even the worst provinces are now practically free from the historic scourge. It was that remarkable man, Dr. Heiser, who not only organized and carried out this great undertaking, but who himself saw to the smallest details. Many times he is known to have carried the loathsome patients in his own arms.

The second problem, that of finding a cure, was not so easily solved. But it has been found, and our nation had the credit of finding it—"the first definite cure ever established," Dr. Heiser says. Two methods were tried out very carefully, both with some success. The first was the x-ray, which brought a marked improvement in most of the cases where it was used, and an apparent cure in one case. The other method was the use of chaulmoogra oil. This remedy had been known and used in the Far East for some time, but it could rarely be given long enough to produce much effect, because it was so unpleasant to swallow. Our doctors, however, devised ways of injecting it, after mixing it with resorcin and camphorated oil, so that there were no ill effects. Already several cures have resulted.

Ten years ago there were forty thousand users of opium in the Islands. In five years that number was reduced ninety-five per cent, and most of those still addicted to the drug are Chinese. In the last few years, moreover, cholera and bubonic plague have been practically wiped out, but, of course, a few other tropical diseases still exist.

The Philippine Assembly recently conceived the brilliant idea of cutting down expenses by halving the health appropriation. Dr. Heiser got permission to speak before them, but instead of talking a few minutes, as they expected, he spoke for three days. He told them that if they did not give him the money he needed for the work, he would be forced to economize by setting free the criminally insane, who, he promised, should be given tags stating that they had been set free by order of the Assembly. Also, he said, he would have to send back many of the lepers to their friends. It proved to be the way to deal with the child-like legislators, who in the end gave him what he wanted. Since that, however, he has resigned, and his loss will be sadly felt. Indeed, there has already been an outbreak of cholera since he left.

Regenerative work among the Filipinos has by no means been confined to their bodies, however, for besides the educational advance that has been made in their schools, which I have mentioned elsewhere, their prisons have become sources of light instead of darkness. It is true that penology in the Philippines has gone ahead with great strides.

In Bontoc, for instance, there is a prison which the commissioner in charge of the province proudly called his "university." Its inmates are men of the mountains. In the old days they would have been sent to Bilibid prison in Manila, where few of them lived over two years. A longer term meant practically a death sentence. This provincial jail is situated in the high and healthy capital of the province, and is kept clean and sanitary by the prisoners themselves. The men are well fed and cared for, and they are taught trades, and made to work at them, too, so that they learn industry along with technical skill.

Bilibid prison is a huge institution. It occupies several acres of land in the heart of the city of Manila, its buildings radiating from a common center, so that the guard in the high tower at the hub can overlook anything that occurs. High walls surround the whole, patrolled by watchful guards and mounted with gatling guns. It is an extraordinary institution, inherited from Spanish rule, but, like everything else, completely changed since then. The wives of men committed there were considered widowed in those days, since so few survived a long term, and were free to marry again. There has been some confusion of late years, because most of the prisoners not only come out alive, but healthier than when they went in. So prison "widows" who remarried found that they had not counted on American methods. Bilibid, though in many ways still rather experimental, is a great success.

There are extensive shops, and the prisoners are kept at work all the time. Some make silverware, carriages, and furniture, while others do the cooking and washing for the prison, make their clothes, and run a laundry, not only for their own use, but for outside custom. Many are employed in road building and on fortifications. Each man learns a trade during his term of imprisonment, and so is better able to earn an honest livelihood than when he entered. I have been told that Bilibid "graduates" are in demand because of their honesty and industry. No better recommendation for a prison could be desired.

Besides the shops, there is a school in which they are taught English. The day we visited the prison we saw a teacher there who had been a guest at the Governor's table, but as he had forged a check he was paying the penalty. Most of the attendants in the up-to-date prison hospital were Spaniards who were in for life sentences and who made very good nurses. Part of this institution is devoted to consumptives, of whom there are so many in the Islands, and they receive treatment according to the best and latest methods.

PENAL COLONY ON THE ISLAND OF PALAWAN.

We were much interested in the kitchens, and the manner in which food was issued to several thousands in only six minutes. It was all wonderfully systematized.

Late in the afternoon we went up into the central tower to watch the "retreat." The prisoners' band, which had played for us as we entered the prison gates, now took its place in the courtyard below and began to play. Out of the workrooms trooped hundreds of convicts, who were searched for hidden implements and then released to take their position in military formation. The different groups marched to their quarters and, standing outside, went through a series of exercises to the music of the band. They seemed to enjoy this very much, and later, still to the music, marched gaily off to get their rations.

A long-term prisoner with two years of good conduct to his credit is given the privilege of going to the penal colony on the island of Palawan. This island is one of the more southern ones, and is the place where the Spanish sent their convicts in the old days. But the present colony, which was established by Governor Forbes, is very different from the former one. It was once a malarial jungle, but now is a healthy, thoroughly up-to-date and successful reform institution.

Our visit to this place was one of the most interesting features of our whole trip. Palawan itself is a curiosity, for it has an underground river which has been explored for two miles beneath a mountain. But the penal settlement is unique.

Leaving the steamer at Puerto Princessa, a quaint little town with charming old Spanish gardens, we were met by a launch which took us up the Iwahig River to the colony. This launch, which was gaily decked with flags, was manned by convicts, the engineer himself being under a sentence of nineteen years for murder. After an hour's sail up the tropical river, we reached our destination. At the wharf we were greeted by Mr. Lamb, superintendent of the colony, a Dominican priest, and a crowd of prisoners who were enjoying a holiday.

We were driven to headquarters, near a pretty plaza with hedges and flowers, surrounded by several two-story barracks built of bamboo and nipa, where the prisoners live. As we walked about the plaza we visited the hospital and the chapel, as well as the main office and the superintendent's house.

The penal settlement is located on a reservation of two hundred and seventy square miles. At the time of our visit there were in all eleven hundred convicts—Filipinos for the most part, with a few Moros—and only three white men to keep them in order. The prisoners had all come from Bilibid prison.

In its management, the colony is somewhat like the George Junior Republic for boys in America. The prisoners elect their own judges and make some of their own laws, subject to the approval of the superintendent. A majority verdict will convict, but the superintendent has the right to veto any measures. Men who break the laws are locked up, but can be released on bail.

The police force is composed of convicts, of course. The chief of police when we were there was a murderer who had earned his pardon but preferred to remain in the settlement. If a prisoner tries to escape he is followed, and occasionally one is shot. The attempt is seldom made, for it is difficult to get away, and the men are, moreover, quite content to live there. Once thirty-five convicts did make a break for liberty, but beyond the confines of the settlement they found themselves in the midst of the savage Mangyans, by whom some were killed. Of the rest, those who were not captured alive returned of their own free will and were consigned again to Bilibid, which is considered a great punishment.

For good behaviour, convicts may earn the right to have a house of their own, with their family, one bull or carabao, and a little farm to cultivate. There were then a hundred and eighty of these farmers, who raised their crops on shares, the government receiving half. They had to report to headquarters by telephone every other day and undergo a weekly inspection as well. Every year they were obliged to plant cocoanuts, which in a few years were expected to bring in large returns. Already great quantities of yams were being shipped to Bilibid, and in a short time enough cattle would be delivered there to supply, in part at least, the meat demand of that prison. The colony suggests the possible solution of the meat question for the American army in the Philippines, as they were successfully raising calves from native cows by Indian bulls.

Although the majority of the prisoners were engaged in farming, they were often given the privilege of selecting the kind of work that they preferred, and were divided accordingly, their hats and the signs on the sleeves of their prison clothes showing what grade of convict they belonged to and what work they did. They were paid in the money of the colony, which was good nowhere else.

There were about forty women on the reservation. The men might marry if they earned the privilege, or if already married, they might have their wives and children come to live with them. There were six marriages the year we were there. After receiving their pardons, they could remain on the island if they wished, their work being credited toward the purchase of their farms, but they had to continue under the laws of the colony.

At the main office we saw four prisoners who were about to be pardoned. Governor Forbes very kindly asked me to hand them their pardons and ask any questions I wished. One, a *bandolero*, or brigand, was small and wizened. Another, who looked much like him, when asked what crime he had committed, laughed and answered, "Bigamy!" A third, a stolid, thickset fellow, had the best face of them all, but showed no emotion whatever when I gave him his pardon. He also had been a brigand.

The convicts gave an exhibition fire drill for us at the barracks. The natives are born climbers, and scramble down the poles with the agility of monkeys. They also play baseball, of course. They are remarkably musical and have a good band.

We had luncheon with Mr. and Mrs. Lamb in their pretty bamboo and nipa cottage. Mrs. Lamb was a frail little woman, but strong in spirit, for she did not seem at all afraid to live in this land of evil men. She told us that the three murderers whom she had as servants were very efficient, and were devoted to her little four-year-old son.

When our visit ended we were driven in a wagon to the river, accompanied by a troop of prisoners who ran alongside shouting good-bys. At the wharf they lined up while Mr. Lamb and the priest bowed us politely aboard the launch.

These intrepid countrymen of ours, who are healing and uplifting a whole people, seem to me to be true missionaries. The time may come when the work which they are doing will set a standard for us stay-at-homes to follow, that is, if we send the right kind of men out there. As the song says,

"Ah, those were the days when the best men won,
The survival of those that were fit—
When the work to be done counted everything,
And politics nary a bit."

CHAPTER VI
DOG-EATERS AND OTHERS

The natives of the Philippines are Malays, as I have said, but they are sometimes classified as Christian, Pagan and Mohammedan Malays. The Christian and educated tribes live near the coast on the lowlands and are called Filipinos. They have intermarried greatly with the Spaniards and Chinese. There are twenty-seven non-Christian tribes in the Islands—about four hundred thousand in number in the Mountain Province of Luzon alone. These hill people are seldom seen, although during the last few years most of the tribes have come under government influence and head-hunting has been more or less given up. These dwellers in the mountains include the aborigines who were driven out of the valleys by the Malays, and also the Malays of the earlier migration, who refused to embrace the Mohammedanism of the Moros of the southern islands or the Christianity of the Spaniards.

We were fortunate in having the opportunity to see some of the dog-eaters and other hill people. Our party was divided, and while several of the men went into the heart of the head-hunting country, the rest of us took the train to Baguio, the mountain capital. What a night it was! The heat was frightful, and swarms of mosquitoes added to the torture. But at sunrise, as I sat on the back platform while the train steamed through rows of cocoanut palms, past little huts and stations, I was reminded of this verse:

"Mighty, luminous and calm
Is the country of the palm,
Crowned with sunset and sunrise,
Under blue unbroken skies,
Waving from green zone to zone,
Over wonders of its own;
Trackless, untraversed, unknown,
Changeless through the centuries."

THE PARTY AT BAGUIO.

Leaving the tropics behind, we climbed up, up among the glorious mountains. At last the train stopped at a little station, and we took the motors that were waiting and went on higher and higher into cloudland, where the tall pines grew and the mountains rose into the sky. We had indeed ascended "into Paradise from Purgatory." As one resident in Manila expressed it: "The heavenly coolness, the sweet pine air and the exquisite scenery give you new life after the years spent in the heat, glare, dust and smells of the lowlands."

We were passing over the far-famed Benguet Road, one of the finest highways in the world, which wound in and out through the gorges of the mountains, repeatedly crossing the river that roared beneath. For twenty miles we zigzagged up the slopes, with widening views of great hills opening before us, and cascades bursting out from beneath the mountains, till we came out on the plateau of Baguio, five thousand feet above the sea.

This road, which has been a favourite theme for discussion by politicians, was opened to traffic in 1905. It is true that the cost of the roadway was beyond what anybody had anticipated, on account of the many bridges that had to be repaired each year after the rainy season, and also after the destructive typhoons that sweep over the island—one in 1911 brought a rainfall of forty-six inches in twenty-four hours—which hurl avalanches of débris from the mountain slopes. For this reason a new road from Bauang to Baguio has been commenced, not nearly so direct but requiring only a few bridges, and it is to be hoped will prove successful and more economical than the other.

Baguio, in the midst of glorious mountain scenery, where the temperature never goes above eighty and the nights are deliciously cool, really is an ideal health resort for a tropical country. The Philippines have Mr. Worcester and Mr. Forbes to thank for this blessing. Government buildings were erected, and the whole force of the government was moved up there for the hot season, with the rich return of the improved health and greater efficiency of the employees. A hospital for tuberculosis was built, and a much needed school for American children, the Jesuit observatory was established, and Camp John Hay was laid out as a permanent military post. Many people bought land and put up little bungalows. A teachers' camp was started by the Bureau of Education for American teachers from all over the Islands, where they had not only rest and recreation but the mental brushing up of good lectures after months in lonely stations.

When the Democratic Administration began its changes in the Philippines, government offices were ordered to be kept in Manila throughout the year, consequently only the higher officials were able to go to Baguio, with a result patent to every one in the lessened efficiency of the force. But within the last two or three years, the Filipinos have come to appreciate the place, which was a revelation to them. Now rich and poor manage to go there, and they have taken possession. The benefits of Baguio and the Benguet Road are felt even in Manila, where Americans are beginning to get fresh garden peas, summer squash, wax beans and real strawberries(!). A friend writes, "If the time ever comes when we can have real cow's milk and cream, then our food will be as good as anywhere in the States."

We had a glorious week at Topside, Governor Forbes's attractive bungalow, and speedily became as enthusiastic in our praises of Baguio as every one else who has ever been there. I rode all day long on Black Crook, the most perfect polo pony in the world, through the mists and the sunlight and into the rainbow shades of the setting sun, where the clouds turned the colour of cockatoos' wings and the tints of the fish from the China Sea.

"Cloud Maidens that float on forever,
Dew-sprinkled, fleet bodies, and fair,
Let us rise from our Sire's loud river,
Great Ocean, and soar through the air
To the peaks of pine-covered mountains
Where the pines hang as tresses of hair."

I played my first polo game at Baguio on the club grounds. Squash Pie, Calico Pie and other delightful names were given to the native ponies, which are small but very strong.

We went to the government stock farm, where they are trying experiments in breeding horses. They had a native pony there that had been well fed and taken care of for some time, in order to show the difference between it and the forlorn animals that one might see anywhere in the towns. The native Spanish pony has greatly degenerated. At this farm they had a beautiful Arabian stallion and a Morgan stallion from Vermont. It is said that the first generation of American horses does well in the Philippines, but after that the climate and the change in food cause them to deteriorate. Besides, they are rather too big for mountain cavalry. The Arabian stallion and the native mare are said to breed the best kind of horse for this country. Black Scotch cattle and Australian cattle, which are raised at the government farm, do well. Sheep do not pay, for, to begin with, there is no market for the wool. Goats do well, and goats' milk is in great demand. The natives use principally the carabao and the native cattle, which look like small Jersey cows but are not very good.

Another day, Mrs. Whitmarsh, from Boston, gave us a tea in a little house hung with orchids and Japanese lanterns, and we visited Mr. Whitmarsh's gold mine. Some of us went on horseback down into the valley to see the tunnels. We washed a pan of ore in the brook and found at the bottom little fine gold specks. The Benguet Igorots have mined gold for centuries.

IGOROT SCHOOL GIRL WEAVING.

At Baguio we visited missionary and government schools and Camp John Hay, where Captain Hilgard gave us a reception. At the government school the Igorot boys are taught, among other things, to make attractive mission furniture, while the girls learn to weave, and very pretty things they make. These girls wear short blue skirts and little jackets, and have their hair in two long black braids that hang on either side of their faces. A Turkish towel, worn as a turban, on which to rest burdens, seemed to be the fashion in head gear with them. Loads are also carried by the Igorots on their backs, hung by straps over the forehead.

It was an Igorot child in this school who wrote the following article upon Mrs. Dickinson's visit at Baguio:

"It was yesterday morning very early when we started from here to the Post Office to meet a lady named Mrs. Dickinson. So early we all went down the brook to take our bath. After we had taken our bath we had breakfast. I was late so Ina scolded me, but I am glad she did it so that some day I won't do it again. Then we were all line up in two by two. When we got up to the Post Office she was not there so we waited for her an hour or two. After waiting for them they arrived suddenly. There were some ladies who accompanied Mrs. Dickinson. We were very much pleased to see her and she was much pleased too. The first time that she came in the Philippine Islands from America and she is soprice (surprised). We sang three songs and the National Anthem and waving our flags on the road. When we finished singing they clapped their hands. I gave her a bouquet of pink flowers. This we did it for our honour of Mrs. Dickinson not because she is more kind or lovely lady but because she is the wife of Mr. Dickinson. This Secretary of War is the leader of those who have authorities. He is responsible of them. After that we came right back. Miss B. came for school. We cleaned the schoolroom and the yard so that they will be so tidy when they come to see the school at three o'clock. We fixed the two bridges and we trimmed the road little bit for their automobiles to dance on. But they left them on the road yonder because they afraid might the bridges will do them damage. So they walked from there to here, and when they went back, they walked from here to there again, making them a journey."

IGOROT OUTSIDE HIS HOUSE.

Doctor White, the missionary at Baguio, and his sister took me one day to the tombs of the Igorots. High on the hills looking toward the sea are great natural rocks with cracks in them, one of which looked like the Sphinx. Here we got off our ponies, tied them, and entered on foot a tangled path leading to a cavern. In the faint light that sifted through we saw a coffin, some baskets and some hats, and farther on, concealed and yet overlooking a fine view, were more wooden coffins. Some of these had fallen apart so that we could see the remains of bones and clothes. When an Igorot dies the body is usually tied in a sitting position on the top of a pole in the house and smoked for several days over a fire built underneath it. Meanwhile, the family kill and cook all the pigs and carabaos and ponies, if the man owned any, and then gather around and have what they call a *cañao*, or feast. Afterward the bones and skulls of the carabaos are hung about the house to show their neighbours what a rich man he was.

Some of us went one day to Mirador, the typhoon station, on a high hill overlooking the sea. It is in charge of a Jesuit priest, who predicts the approach of typhoons and puts up storm signals, in this way preventing great loss of life. We were shown the instruments, which give warning of earthquakes as well as typhoons, and given sherry that was fifty years old, delicious cake, and flowers from his garden, and we saw his goats climbing up the steep crags. He told us with a chuckle that he had traded his dog to an Igorot for a cow.

On Sunday we visited the dog market, but alas! we saw no dogs, as on account of cholera in the vicinity, it was forbidden to sell any. A few days before we had seen several men leading a number of lean and lanky ones along the road, and these were all for sale, to be killed and eaten. Long-haired canines are not popular, the short-haired kind are preferred.

Vice-Governor Gilbert had a cañao, or feast, in front of his house one morning. A line of partly dressed dog-eaters arrived, bowing as they passed. They proved to be the chiefs or head men, who had put on what clothes they possessed for this occasion. They were brown, bare-legged men with gee strings, as they call the woven cloth hanging about their waists. Some had coats on, but nothing underneath, and only an old hat to complete the costume.

The Benguet Igorots, or dog-eaters, are small but strong, and remind one of our American Indians. They are peaceful farmers now, but in days gone by they fought their neighbours on the north, and so lances and shields are still to be found among them. "The first American civil provincial government established in the Philippines was in Benguet, and governmental control has been continuously exercised there since November 23, 1900. They are gladly availing themselves of the opportunity now afforded for the education of their children, but insist that this education be practical."

In order to show the progress that had been made in the Philippines, a party of Igorots were brought to the St. Louis Exposition. Part of the exhibit was a model schoolroom. Visitors were amazed at the bright, eager little children, and at their keen interest in their lessons. But they were even more amazed one day to see these same model pupils when a dog suddenly barked outside. For the school simply went to pieces, the children making for the nearest door. The last seen of them, they were in full cry after the unfortunate dog.

Although we found the dog-eaters interesting, there are other tribes of far greater interest, such as the Negritos, the warlike Ilongots and the Tingians, as well as the people of the Bashee rocks of the north, who are hardly ever seen.

The Negritos are diminutive and uncivilized black people who live to-day in a few mountain areas. They are the aborigines of the islands in this part of the world, and are as primitive as the Australian blacks, having no social or political organization but that of the family. They live in hollow trees or under little lean-tos of grass and brush, and subsist principally by hunting and fishing, at which they are very expert. Their weapons are poisoned arrows and the blow gun. The poison, which is made either from the leaf of a tree or from decomposed meat, is placed in the arrow-head of hollow bone. On striking, it injects the poison into the flesh as a hypodermic needle would do, quickly resulting in death.

The only agricultural implement of the Negritos is a pointed stick hardened in the fire. To prepare the ground for cultivation, on the space they wish to clear they girdle the trees, which will soon die. They are then set on fire and the ashes distributed over the soil. Later, holes are made with the pointed sticks, and *camotes*, sugar-cane and tobacco are planted.

These people are very timid, and if their suspicions are aroused in the slightest manner, they immediately disappear into the forest. Very little success has attended any effort to civilize them. Their religion is nature worship with many local divinities and good and bad spirits of all sorts.

They ornament their bodies with scar patterns, made by cutting the skin with sharp pieces of bamboo and then rubbing dirt into the wounds. In this respect they are like no other tribes in the Islands but resemble the most primitive of the native Africans, who also make scar patterns. The men often shave the crowns of their heads in order, they say, "to let the heat out." The Negritos, like the Bagobos of the south, sometimes point their front teeth, but not by filing them as one might suppose. They are chopped off with a bolo.

Worcester says the Negritos "believe that each family must take at least one head per year or suffer misfortune in the form of sickness, wounds, starvation or death." Heads are buried in the ground under the "houses" of the men who take them.

In regard to the Tingians of northern Luzon I also quote from Worcester, who has given us the most reliable account of them:

"The women of this tribe ornament their arms with a series of bracelets and armlets, which often extend from wrist to shoulder. They constrict the middle of the forearm during early girlhood and continue to wear tight armlets on the constricted portion throughout life, so that their forearms become somewhat hourglass-shaped, this being considered a mark of great beauty in spite of the unsightly swelling of the wrists which results....

"Their cooking utensils are taken to the river and scrubbed with sand after every meal. If a wife offers her husband dirty or soggy rice to eat, the offense is said to afford ground for divorce....

ILONGOT IN RAIN-COAT AND HAT OF DEERSKIN.

"When a man dies, whether his death be natural or due to violence, the other members of his family repair by night to some village of their enemies, cut pieces from their turbans, and throw them down on the ground. This is interpreted as an intimation that they will return and take heads sometime within six months, and they believe that the dead man knows no peace until this is done."

The Ilongots, who live in the province of Nueva Viscaya, are especially wild and great head-hunters. They are striking figures in their deerskin rain-coats. No young man can take to himself a bride until he has brought back a head to prove his prowess. The favourite time for these gruesome excursions of the tribe is when the blossoms of the fire tree show their red beacons on the mountain sides. As an especial mark of beauty and valour, because a good deal of pain has to be endured in the process, the men cut off the upper front teeth on a line with the gums.

Woe betide the man who rides a white horse into the Ilongot country, for above all things white hair is desired, and unless he stands guard over it, he will find its mane missing and its tail cropped to the skin.

Most of the mountain people still retain their ancient myths and traditions. Even among these Ilongots there are tales of the long ago when they came across a "great water" to their present abode. This, of course, merely explains the general migration of the Malay tribes. By the way, this Malay migration is still in progress, and is exemplified by the Samal boatmen who come from Borneo and further south in Malaysia to the southern Philippines.

All the wild people have customs of their own, which distinguish them, especially the manner in which they cut their hair and wear their loin cloths. They have slightly different methods of fighting, some fighting singly with a kind of sword, others in pairs with spears and arrows, while the sword is used only to decapitate the fallen enemy. Others display considerable ability in organization and operate large bands, under especially designated chiefs. All are very fond of dancing and have different dances to represent war, love and the chase.

ILONGOTS RETURNING FROM THE CHASE.

They have their own explanations for everything, and their stories about the creation of the various birds and animals are quite interesting and not unlike those found among some tribes of aborigines in North America. One of them relates that one day the Creator was making the different birds. Before him lay bodies, wings, necks, heads and feet. He would begin with the body and build it up with appropriate parts, so that it could apply itself to the purpose for which it was intended. In every case, the Creator was particular not to put on the wings before the bird was complete, for fear that it would take flight in an imperfect condition. One day while he was engaged in making an especially fine specimen of the feathered world, the evil spirit approached and engaged the Good Spirit in conversation. Ordinarily he would have attacked the Evil One and quickly put him to flight, but as the bird was nearly finished and already imbued with the spark of life he wished to complete him. But the Creator's anger that the Evil One should overlook his work, became so great that, without thinking, he put on the wings before the legs had been fitted. Instantly the bird flew off. In haste the Creator grabbed the first pair of legs he could lay his hands on and threw them at it. They attached themselves exactly where they struck the bird, near the tail. This is the reason, so the story goes, that the loon's legs are so far back that he cannot walk in an upright position on land. His peculiarly sad cry is a lament because he must stay in the water practically all the time and cannot enjoy himself on land as other good birds do.

Many of the people who live along the foot of the mountain ranges, although Christianized sufficiently to contribute to the Roman Catholic churches, still retain many of their aboriginal customs, especially those pertaining to marriage, birth and death.

Beyond the shores of Luzon, stretching northward for nearly two hundred miles, is an interesting archipelago of diminutive islands known as the Bashee Rocks, the Batan and the Babuyan Islands.[19] The natives still retain many of the characteristics which were observed by Dampier in his visit to these islands in the seventeenth century.

The inhabitants of the Batan group are like those living on the Japanese island of Botel Tobago, which is only sixty miles north of our most northern possession.[20] No missionaries or other persons had been allowed by the natives to land on their shores until a few Japanese police arrived in 1909. They are mentioned in passing because they are a present-day example of what the people in the northern islands of the Philippine group were before the coming of the white men and the friars. Their dwellings are very peculiar. Each family has a stone-paved court surrounded by a low wall of stone. Within this enclosure they have three houses: one with its sides sunk down into the ground, in order to give protection from high winds; one with ordinary walls for use during normal weather; and a third built on poles about ten feet above the ground for use during the hot season. From these elevated houses a constant watch is maintained for schools of fish. The people are expert fishermen and make excellent nets, and they have beautiful boats with high bows and sterns.

In Dampier's day the people were friendly and hospitable, as they are at the present time. They valued iron more than gold, and gladly exchanged it for iron. The ancient diggings are still to be seen, but the "pay dirt" is of such a low grade that it is not worth while to work it. The precious metal is washed out by the natives in cocoanut shells, which take the place of our prospectors' "gold pan." Many gold ornaments of attractive design are still to be found in these islands. Some of those taken from graves remind one strongly of Chaldean work.

The graves of the ancient inhabitants were placed high upon the mountains, some near the smoking craters of the volcanoes, others on the crests of the non-volcanic hills. It is supposed that the graves near the smoking craters were those of persons who had a bad reputation in the community, while those on the tops of the ridges contained the bodies of the good, and that by this method of burial the ideas of heaven and hell were carried out in a practical manner. The bodies were placed in *ollas*, or earthenware jars, some of which had a high glaze and were profusely ornamented. The corpse was inserted into the jar in a sitting position, and the orifice was sealed by placing an inverted olla over the mouth of the first. These jars were then placed on end and a small pyramid of stones built around them, on the top of which a little tree was planted. A number of these graves ranged around the edge of a smoking sulphur crater are an uncanny sight, which the natives take good care to avoid.

The women of the Batan Islands, when walking or working out of doors, wear a distinctive headdress, consisting of a long grass hood, which stretches from the forehead to below the hips. It protects the head and back from the sun, wind and rain, so that it is worn at all times and in all seasons. It is one of the most original and useful of all primitive garments.

WOMAN OF THE BATAN ISLANDS WITH GRASS HOOD.

During the dry season but little rain falls in these islands, and as there are few streams or springs, every means is employed to catch the least drop. Even the trees in the yards have pieces of rattan twisted around their trunks and larger branches, to make the water drop off into earthen jars.

During the autumn migration of hawks and eagles from the north, men are stationed on the thatched roofs of the high dwellings to seize the birds by the feet as soon as they alight. Great numbers are caught in this manner every year and form quite an element of the food supply.

Many of the islands are excellent places for the production of cattle. Itbayat Island, unique because its shores are higher than the interior, has many thousand head of excellent cattle. The coast is so precipitous that when they are exported they have to be lowered to the water's edge by means of a block and tackle, as at Tangier. They then have to swim out to the waiting ship, where they are hoisted by their horns to the deck.

Another of the cattle islands is called Dalupiri. This beautiful spot was given in its entirety to Aldecoa and Company of Manila by the Spanish government. In fact, when the United States first took possession of the Philippines, this company claimed sovereignty over the island, but this, of course, was not recognized by the United States Government. The cattle that are pastured here are a cross between the black Spanish bulls of fighting lineage and the humped cattle of India. Great care is taken that the stock be well kept up, and for this purpose there is a constant weeding out of undesirables. The method in which this is done is both interesting and very exciting. The cattle roam at will and are very wild and hard to approach; as a result they have to be hunted with great care. About twenty men are employed in their capture, all of whom are mounted on hardy little horses. Four of them are lassoers and the rest huntsmen. The lassos are nooses attached to the ends of bamboo poles about twelve feet long. The rope from the noose, to the length of about twenty-five feet, is coiled around the bamboo pole and tied to it four feet from the lower end. When the lasso is thrown over an animal's head the pole is dropped by the rider, the rope unwinds and drags the pole along the ground, until it catches on a rock or a bush and stops the mad career of the animal.

"We started out early one morning," Major Mitchell writes me, "to cut several young bulls out of a herd of about five hundred cattle. Led by the manager of the island, we galloped over the rough surface of the coral-bound hilltops and through deep, waving grass until one of the huntsmen signaled that the herd was in sight. A careful inspection was made of the herd with a telescope, and the animals for capture were selected and carefully pointed out to the lassoers, who immediately took up their posts in concealment beside a little plain. The huntsmen then proceeded under cover to points around the herd which would enable them to drive the cattle on to the little plain where the lassoers could get in their work. After a wait of about a half hour, the horn of the chief huntsman pealed forth and was answered by the yells of his companions; the herd, unable to go in another direction, dashed for the little plain, followed by its pursuers. Crouching behind some low bushes the lassoers waited until the cattle, now in full stampede, had come within fifty yards, when in a twinkling they dashed into the midst of the galloping herd.

"After a terrific race one lasso held true on a fine young bull, while the rest scampered off into the ravines and water courses. The dragging bamboo pole soon brought him to a stop, and after several charges at his captors, two more lassos were placed on him, and he was securely fastened and dragged to a tree, against which his head was tied. A little saw was produced from somewhere, and his gallant horns were cut off short. An old, sedate carabao, who seemed to be perfectly at home, made his appearance, the young bull was tied to the carabao's harness and towed off toward the corral. At first he tried frantically to gore the carabao, but as his horns had been removed no harm resulted. The carabao did not mind it in the least but continued tranquilly on his way. Three more bulls were captured on that day; each furnished exceedingly fast and interesting sport. I have seen mounted work of a great many kinds, such as pig sticking, stag hunting, and hunting of many kinds of game, including our own fox hunting and polo, but never have I seen any mounted work which required more dash, nerve, good judgment and endurance than that displayed by these herdsmen of the northern islands."

Although these islands are bounded on the north by the Balintan Channel, through which some of the shipping passes from America to the southern part of China, they are seldom visited. This is because, as I have said before, there are no ports, not even good anchorages. During the typhoon season they are exposed to the full force of these great hurricanes, while the waters are infested with hidden rocks and coral ledges. The U. S. cruiser *Charleston* ran aground on a coral reef east of the island of Camaguin in 1900 and sank immediately. During the Russo-Japanese war the fleet of the Russian Admiral Rojesvenski passed on either side of Batan Island. The Japanese had observers on the summit of Mt. Iraya on this island, who are supposed to have signaled by heliograph to Mt. Morrison in Formosa of the coming of the fleet. The great armada could be seen from this mountain for more than one hundred miles.

CHAPTER VII
AMONG THE HEAD-HUNTERS

When the Americans first came to the Philippines, most of the mountain country could be reached only on foot over dangerous trails. Very large tracts were unexplored, and the head-hunting tribes, who are found nowhere but in this northern part of Luzon, pillaged the neighbouring towns. A state of order has now been established, except in parts of Kalinga and Apayao.

The Mountain Province, the home of the head-hunters, includes the sub-provinces of Benguet, Lepanto, Amburayan, Bontoc, Ifugao, Kalinga and Apayao. The officers of the provinces are a governor, a secretary-treasurer, a supervisor in charge of the road and trail work and the construction of public buildings, and seven lieutenant governors. All these officers are appointed by the governor general. They live on horseback, undergo great hardships and also take great risks.

The manners and customs of these head-hunting tribes differ somewhat. Each one, for instance, has a different mode of treating the captured head when it is brought in, but all celebrate a successful hunt with a cañao, or festival. The Ifugaos place the head upon a stake and hold weird ceremonial dances around it, followed by speech making and the drinking of *bubud*, as they call their wine; afterward the skull of the victim is utilized as a household ornament. Venison and chicken are served at such feasts and the large fruit-eating bats, which are considered delicacies. If one of the tribe has been so unfortunate as to have his head taken, they berate the spirit at the funeral, "asking him why he had been careless enough to get himself killed."

The most picturesque of the head-hunting tribes that my husband saw were the Kalingas, who are different from all other natives of Luzon. It is said that the Spaniards took fifteen hundred Moros into this part of the country more than a hundred years ago, so they may have founded this tribe. At all events, the Kalingas are superbly developed, tall and slight, some of the men having handsome and almost classical features.

Neither the men nor the women cut the hair, which, in the case of the men, is banged in front and tied up with rags behind, some wearing nets to keep it out of their eyes. Although the women have abundant hair they use "switches," into which they stick beautiful feathers. The men also decorate themselves in the same way. On the back of the head they often wear little caps woven of beautifully stained rattan and covered with agate beads, and these are used as pockets in which small articles are carried. Great holes are pierced in the lobes of their ears, into which are thrust wooden ear plugs, with tufts of red and yellow worsted. Almost every Kalinga woman wears a pair of heavy brass ear ornaments and sometimes a solid piece of mother-of-pearl cut like a figure eight.

The Kalingas are particularly warlike, their very name meaning "enemy" or "stranger," and endeavours to bring them under government control were begun only a few years ago. There are still some *rancherias* which the lieutenant governor has not yet visited, as it seemed best to wait and bring the people to terms by peaceful means.

While we were enjoying ourselves at Baguio, the Secretary of War, Governor Forbes, Secretary Worcester, General Edwards, and my husband started north into the mountains to see some of the strange tribes that were gathering from far and wide to meet the great *Apo*, or chief, as they called Secretary Dickinson. I give the account of the trip in my husband's own words:

On Saturday night, July 31st, after the Assembly baile, we motored to the docks and went aboard the transport *Crook* for the trip northward. We were made very comfortable on this big transport, with deck cabins, but we all slept on the open deck by preference and had a pleasant run till in the morning we were entering Subig Bay, a splendid vast harbour between great mountains, the narrow entrance guarded by Isola Grande. Here we landed and visited the batteries, and although it was a small island it was a stewing hot walk about it—especially as the Secretary sets a great pace—till a torrential shower came up and drove us to the commanding officer's house, where we had a bite of breakfast—and all the breakfasts at the posts which we have visited have been so good!

General Duvall had come up from Manila on his yacht *Aguila*, and on board of her we crossed the bay to Olongapo, where there is the present naval station. The great hulk of the famous floating dock *Dewey* was looming up there, just floated again after her mysterious sinking which, even now, they do not seem to be able to explain.

The guard was out with the band, and the honours were paid and the marines paraded, but soon another severe tropical storm broke, and drove some of us back to the ship while the others went on to another breakfast at the Officers' Club. This storm suggested a typhoon, but there had been no warning from the Jesuit observatory at Manila, and so we rejoined the *Crook* out by Isola Grande and went to sea without fear.

This is the rainy and typhoon season but the warnings of severe storms are so carefully given that they have lost their terrors now-a-days; and this year, so far, there hasn't been a disturbance, much to our comfort, as it has permitted the carrying out of all our plans. It is a most unusual thing for such good weather to continue. The hot season is over, and this is called the intermediate, but it is the time of rains on this coast, the seasons differing slightly on the different coasts and in the different islands. So all that night we cruised up the coast through showers of rain and lightning, passing by Bolinao Light, which we had first sighted as we approached the Philippines.

Before daylight we stopped off Tagudin, and through the darkness could be seen the dim shadow of land and mountains, and a light burning on the beach as a beacon. With dawn we saw a wonderful tropical shore develop before us, of low land fringed with palm, surrounded by beautiful mountain ranges, a tiny village on the beach, and a crowd of people gathered together. Soon a surf-boat put out and brought aboard the governors of the nearby provinces—Early and Gallman, brave, ready men, who have taken these wild people in hand and become demi-gods among them—and after a bite of breakfast we were all taken ashore through the surf, very handily, and the Secretary was welcomed by a native band and the chief men of the neighbourhood and crowds of half naked natives.

The Ilocanos of the northwest coast of Luzon are a fine, kindly race, but there had also come down from the interior a lot of small brown men to pack in our baggage, Bontoc Igorots, head-hunters and dog-eaters, of whom we were to see more in their own country. These little fellows at first seemed like dwarfs; but soon after, as we saw them better, they proved small but well formed and well nourished, strong, gentle little people. They ran forward and seized our packages and disappeared down the trail in a wild, willing manner. Off they trotted while we were packed into carromatos, dragged by weedy, diminutive native horses, which are wonderfully powerful for their size. We went, after greeting the people, off down the trail, through the outskirts of Tagudin (we didn't go into the town, which was somewhat to one side, as there had been some cholera there), with its nipa houses of plaited grass, perched up above the ground, many decorated in honour of the occasion. We rattled along an excellent road (for we have certainly done wonders in road-building here), past paddy fields, where the slow carabao grazed with little children perched on their backs, past troops of natives, with their loads, standing alongside.

Governor General Forbes had made the most wonderful preparations for the trip. It was the first time that any American officials (only Insular officials previously) had gone in to these wild people, and of course the Secretary is the highest in rank that can visit the Islands since he is the one through whom the President governs the Philippines and the President can never come. The trip was unique and all the arrangements were extraordinary. For a new trail had been planned into the mountains but was not due to be done for eight months, and yet thousands of these wild men had been called in and helped to finish the road so much the more quickly (for we were the first party to pass over it, and some of the bridges had only been finished the night before we passed), eagerly and willingly, when they were told that the great Apo was coming in to visit them. Forbes had sent to Hongkong for some rick'shaws and had had men trained to pull and push them, but these had not stood the test well and we didn't have the need or the chance to use them; he also had had palanquin chairs brought over from China and men taught in a way to carry them, and these we did use on some of the steep descents. But we rode horses, excellent ones, from Forbes's own stable, almost all the way.

Every three kilometers, companies of Igorots and Ifugaos were stationed to act as *cargadores* and rush along the baggage by relays, and this they did with shouts and cheers as quickly as we traveled. Tiffin and breakfasts had been prepared all along the way. Every eventuality had been anticipated, and it was really too well done, for it made our traveling seem so easy that we had to think hard to realize into what out-of-the-way places we were going. A few days before it would have been necessary to work our way over the perpendicular old trails, with difficulty finding bearers for our packs, and we would have been compelled to carry our own food, a severe trip and a hard undertaking. We went in absolutely unarmed and without escort, and yet nearly every native that we saw, after we reached the hills, carried his spear and head ax; but there wasn't a suggestion of danger. People were brought together on this occasion from different tribes who two years ago would have killed each other at sight, and yet to-day were dancing with each other.

We were accompanied by the governors of the sub-provinces as we passed through them, and an unarmed orderly and Sergeant Doyle, who had charge of Governor Forbes's horses, and generally by a shouting horde of natives. The Secretary proved a wonder; well mounted, as he was, he led on at a great pace, till it seemed a sort of endurance test. I was more than pleased to find that I stood it as I did, for we traveled four days out of the five for forty miles a day, and rode most of it a-horseback. I came out finally in much better form than when I went in.

And so, from the beach where we landed, the carromatos carried us across the low coast plain, over new bridges on which the inscriptions stated that they had been finished for the passage of the Secretary and his party, and under triumphal arches made of bamboo which welcomed him; all the natives whom we passed saluted, and many wished to shake hands or only touch the hand as we passed, till we came into the foothills, and over them into a little village of nipa huts among the bamboo and tropical trees, where we found our horses waiting. Here we mounted and started off at a good pace over the well built road that trailed around cliff and crag as we worked into the mountains, a procession, a cavalcade, winding in and out. We traveled along the valley of a river, that later became a gorge with steep cliffs and precipitous sides; all the natives were out to greet the Secretary; and finally we came to a tiny village where we had a drink of refreshing cocoanut water, all the people standing about or hanging out of the windows of the simple houses, which looked very clean and neat. We trailed on along the narrow road, cut into the rock in many places, really a remarkable road, and up the gorge with the rushing river below us. The mountains rose high and opened up in lovely velvety greens, and shaded away into the blues of distance. We stopped at a little native rest house, above a ford in the river, where we found a luncheon prepared for us, but it was a hurried luncheon, and on we went climbing a winding trail that zigzagged up the steep mountainside, through tropical tangle of bamboo and fern and great overhanging trees with trailing parasites—the ghost tree, the hard woods, and some with a beautiful mauve flower at the top that even Mr. Worcester couldn't tell me the name of (he said he had been so busy inventing names for the birds that he hadn't had time yet to find names for trees). And below the views opened up wider and more splendid, and range on range of mountains rose above each other, while the precipices grew deeper and more terrifying.

And suddenly, as we came to a turn in the trail, there appeared above us a most picturesque sight against the skyline, some Ifugao warriors, lithe, beautifully formed men, whose small size was lost in their symmetry, with spears in their hands, turbans of blue wrapped about their heads, and loin cloths of blue with touches of red and yellow in their streaming ends that hung like an apron before and like a tail behind; their handsome brown bodies like mahogany. They had belts made of round shells from which hung their bolos. These were the head men of a company of Ifugaos who had come this far to greet the party and they stood so gracefully on the point above us; and around the turn we found the rest of the band, stunning looking fellows, standing at attention in line behind their lances, which were stuck in a row in the ground. Here we had another tiffin, while these warriors seized and scampered off with our luggage.

From this time on, as we traveled, we found reliefs of these picturesque people, waiting their turn at carrying, and then all would join in the procession, and shouting a cheer like American collegians, their war cry, they would rush on and frighten us to death with the risk of going over the steep places. Away off in the distance, reëchoing through the valleys, we could hear the cheers and cries, very musical, of others of our party as they traveled along. Soon we began to be greeted by the tom-toms of natives who had come out to honour the Secretary, and by their singing as we approached, and then they would dance round in a strange way as we passed on.

The Ifugaos had come to meet the Secretary from several days' journey away, mostly through Bontoc Igorot country, all armed, and yet there hadn't been a sign of trouble. And these Ifugaos, who two years ago were wild head-hunters, have been brought into wonderful control by their governor, Gallman. There are some one hundred and twenty thousand of these picturesque people, among whom head-hunting is now nearly stamped out; though there are sporadic cases doubtless. These little savages, too, appear most gentle and tractable, most willing and laughing, in the rough tumbling of the trail; and they have proved very clever, for they were the builders of the roads over which we traveled (we were told that they could drill rock better than Americans, on a few months' practice, and that they have sat for a few days and watched Japanese bricklayers set brick, and then done it as well as the Japanese). But indeed their *sementeras*—their paddy fields—their terracing, which they have practised for hundreds of years, is the most wonderful in the world, and there is nothing even in Japan to compare with their work of this kind. Their great game of head-hunting has taught them cleverness, and they are full of snap and go.

The Ifugao is a great talker and has all the gestures of an orator. When he begins a speech he first gives a long call to attract attention, then climbs a stand fifteen feet high by means of a ladder. He generally begins his remarks by stating that he is a very rich man, and goes on to praise himself and his tribe, and at the end of his harangue he often himself leads off in the applause by loudly clapping his hands. He has become a fine rifleman and is a fearless fighter. In clout, coat and cap, and a belt of ammunition, with legs bare, he travels incredible distances and makes a good constabulary soldier. The Governor General is anxious to form them into a militia, but they lose their grip, we were told, when they are taken down from the hills to the plain.

CONSTABULARY SOLDIERS.

And so we went on up to over four thousand feet, to where the pass broke through the mountain, and there before us was a vast valley with a splendid plain beyond, and in the middle of it, on a prominence, we could see Cervantes, where we were to stop our first night. It seemed so near and yet proved many miles away as we traced our way down the steep coasts of the valley and the view of the plain below widened and the ranges of mountains beyond rose into finer heights. We twisted and trailed zigzag down the pine-clad slopes, for the change of vegetation (due to the mountain range, which divided a different climate on either side of it) in passing over the ridge had been remarkable, and though we had seen rare orchids and begonias as we mounted, we descended from the same height through pine and pasture.

When finally we reached the plateau and had crossed a river bed we were met by the people of the village of Cervantes—many girls in gay dress riding astride on their midget ponies, and men and boys on their rugged little mounts. These escorted the party under the triumphal arches into the grass streets of the pretty village, where the simple public buildings were decorated, and the local band played, till we finally were taken to the houses where we were to spend the night, the Secretary and the Governor and Clark and myself going to the Lieutenant Governor's. He was married to a Filipina wife. And here I must say that we met several of these Filipina wives of white men, and they had most perfect manners and self possession and real grace (and this one was a good cook). The house was a best class native house and more comfortable than we had anticipated, though there were sounds and smells that rather disturbed us. There was a reception and baile at the municipal building in the evening, where we had to go and dance a rigodon, each partnered off with some dainty little Filipina lady. And then we did hurry home to rest, for we had been up since half after four that morning and were to start next morning a little after five.

The next day's trail was very fine, for we started off over a river which we crossed on a flying bridge, a swinging car on a cable, while the horses were forded; and then we had splendid but slow climbing up the gorge of one river after another, coasting the mountainside, where we could see the mark of the trail many miles ahead above us and part of our procession trailing along in single file or rushing along with distant shout, as the little willing native cargadores carried their loads up and up. Above us rose Mount Data, with its mysterious waterfall that seems to come right out of its peak, and clouds circled about us, and below the valleys streaked away into the distance and the ranges rose higher and higher, and the play of light and shadow was beautiful on the greens and grays and browns and blues of the distances. We began to see rancherias, the native villages, perched up on the hills, the thatched roofs like haystacks, with blue smoke at times coming through; and paddy fields began to climb the upper valleys in their terraces, with the pale green rice, and fringes of the banana palm of which the hemp is made. In places the red croton was planted on the terraces for luck, and in the ravines which we crossed there were cascading falls and pools.

We rose higher and higher over another range, and at the tip-top of the trail another group of Igorots were dancing and playing their tom-toms as we passed, and rushed alongside to touch fingers. Soon we passed through a village built in a stony gorge where a river ran down. The houses consisted of conical thatched roofs supported on four wooden piers with ladders leading up into the roofs where the people lived. The foundations were terraced in stone and the paths were stone-terrace, and it all looked very neat and clean. On our way back we stopped for tiffin at this same village and had the women come and show us how they weave, for it was a place famed for its weaving. This time our tiffin was farther on, at a rest-house with a splendid view, and it had been laid out so prettily with temporary flower beds and bamboo arches. The Belgian priest from a town nearby had come to join us at luncheon, and although he spoke no English I had a pleasant time with him in French, for he proved to be a sort of relative of our cousins the de Buisserets; his name was Padre Sepulchre, one of a band of Belgians belonging to no order but educated highly for missionary priesthood, who have been sent out, since our occupation, by the Pope, and many of whom are rich and gentlemen born. This one had already in two years spent some twenty thousand dollars gold of his own money in his town. Another such missionary we met at Bontoc, and several at other places, and all are said to do good work.

RICE TERRACES.

We started off after tiffin on the long trail that wound down the gorge of El Chico de Cagayan River, on our way to Bontoc. Villages became more numerous and were very picturesque, on the spurs of mountain above the river, or embowered in coffee trees, where the mountain coasts were patched with pineapple plantations. And the paddy fields grew in terrace after terrace, most splendid engineering by these primitive people, rising above each other up into the clouds, fitting into the contours of the mountainsides, the terrace walls overgrown with green, and the pale green paddy within, and little cascades carrying the water down from terrace to terrace, most lovely, like some great hanging gardens; little brown people were stooping at work in them, all naked, but with their clothes covered by leaves and balanced on their heads, to be kept dry; for there were showers and cloud effects that added to the beauty of the panorama as we passed. The terraces add beauty and interest to the eye by their succession of levels, and as we traveled into the country they became more frequent and complete. Curiously enough, the Bontoc Igorots have forest laws and a forest service of their own. The mountainsides of their rough country are sparsely timbered with pine, which has grown very scarce near some of the larger settlements. Forests in the vicinity of such settlements are divided up into small private holdings claimed by individuals, whose right thereto is recognized by the other members of the tribe. In many places it is forbidden to cut trees until they have reached a large size, although the lower branches are constantly trimmed off and used for firewood. Forest fires are kept down to facilitate reforestation, and young trees are planted. Such foresight on the part of a primitive people is certainly unusual.

So we trailed all day, till toward half after five we turned a point and came to Bontoc, after a procession of natives had come streaming out some miles up the gorge to meet the party. Bontoc is the capital of the Mountain Province and was the goal of our journey.

The native town is very dirty and is acknowledged to be one of the worst of the native villages; in the more savage places the towns are said to be cleaner. We walked through it, where the terraced stone walks pass by stone pits where the pigs wallow, and by thatched houses which have no exit for the smoke and so are filthy and in dreadful condition. We saw the communal shacks in which the unmarried and widowed members live with their peculiar rights, and the sties where the old men resort to talk, and we stood outside the wretched place where the skulls are kept, and some heads, all black and smoked, were brought out in a basket from the secret recesses for us to see.

IFUGAO COUPLE.

Some of these Bontoc Igorots are skilful smiths, and they make excellent earthen pots and clay pipes. They have interesting athletic sports of their own and take to those of the Americans. They are especially fond of beads, which are wound in their hair or hung about the neck, and greatly value large white stones, caring little for agates, so highly prized by the Kalingas.

Into Bontoc for this great occasion had been brought warriors and women from the Kalingas and Ifugaos, with Igorots from about, some from a distance of several days' travel; and for the first time these warring tribes, who only two years before were taking each other's heads, came peacefully together, and watched each other with as much interest as they watched us.

The adventures of the American lieutenant governors read like romances, and here they were before us with their following: the Kalingas more dangerous and warlike than the Ifugaos, and the Ifugaos more picturesque and interesting than the Igorots, and all together making a never-to-be-forgotten scene.

There were, too, several small companies of native constabulary, for these hill men make splendid soldiers and take great pride in their arms and uniform, and have proved loyal to the death. All the different tribes and the constabulary had turned out to receive the Secretary, and it was a vociferous and noisy yelling crowd that streamed about in irregular procession. We were, some of us, taken to a government house that was comfortable, and took our meals at a club which the officials have built and which is quite pathetically complete, and that evening we did little before turning in—the first evening since we had landed in the Islands when we were able to turn in at a reasonable hour with the prospect of sleeping as late as we pleased next day.

Next day was a day of festivities, a cañao, for from morning till night there was dancing by these fantastic peoples, whom so few white men have ever seen. We were waked early enough, alas! by the *ganzas*—the tom-toms— and there were parades of the different tribes through the town. A small grandstand had been erected in the plaza, and there we stood with the Secretary and the few white teachers and the missionaries from about, while the procession was reviewed.

The constabulary came first, dressed only in loin cloths of different colours below the waist, but with the regulation khaki uniform blouse and cap above. They are officered by Americans and a few natives, and are most military, notwithstanding the strange appearance of their bare legs. Some companies were very well drilled, and they gave exhibitions of different manuals as well as any regular white soldiers might have done.

The wild Kalingas came past next, most picturesque, with their feather headdresses of red and yellow, and spears and head axes, and their brightly coloured loin cloths, and the women in scant but gay garments, and not at all ashamed in their nakedness. And these gave their characteristic dances, with outstretched arms, hopping and prancing about in a circle, all the time looking down into the center of the circle about which they dance (where the head of the decapitated is supposed to be). There were innumerable tom-toms, which they play with variations, so as to make much rhythm and movement, and the women joined in the dancing, more moderately, some with big cigars in their mouths and looking extremely indifferent. Then, when they danced in a circle, some would prance into the center with shield and ax and pretend attacks upon each other, and leap about and grow excited; and this sort of thing they kept up all day (and part of the night, too) off and on.[21]

The Ifugaos followed and passed by, and gave their dances, which are the same with a difference, but each was ended with a mighty shout, after which one of the head men would step forward and deliver a rattling speech, and they greeted the Secretary variously but cordially—for they like our American rule, indeed, they have never had any other, for the Spaniards never attempted to come in and control them.

IFUGAO HEAD DANCE.

Then the Bontoc Igorots followed and gave exhibitions with noisy demonstrations, and two *presidentes*, or chiefs, who six months before were trying to kill each other, danced and pranced together, while the tom-toms beat and others hopped and circled round. Most of the men were tattooed, each tribe in its own peculiar manner, certain marks indicating that their bearer had killed his man and taken a head—some bore marks of many heads; one man dancing was known to have taken seventeen. Many of the women, too, were tattooed with a feather-like pattern.

And so the dances went on. In some the participants postured fighting and then represented wounded men; in others all were head men together; some were rapid in motion, some slow, but all had real grace, that grace of the wild man; and all were finely formed and well-nourished and healthy looking. When the dancing was over, the groups of savages in their fantastic dress squatting around the plaza behind their spears stuck in the ground, with bolo and head-ax and tom-tom, and the women standing about, made a wonderful scene.

After the dances and speeches the head men came up to the Secretary and handed him weapons as gifts, sometimes their own, with which they had often fought. Mr. Dickinson, of course, received the chiefs and the head men and women afterward, and presented them with shells and blankets and plumes in return. The bartering among them was rather amusing, as they tried to exchange what they had received and didn't want.

WEAPONS OF THE WILD TRIBES.

At the club in the evening of the second day, they gave us a remarkable dinner; all the Americans in the district were present; and the few Filipinos entertained us at a baile, and so our day was finished.

We started out at daylight next morning and hiked back by the same trail; but the views seemed finer in their repetition than even when we first passed through them. We had had most superb weather, although it was the rainy season, and had enjoyed the grand panoramas to the full; but the last afternoon it came on to pour down in torrents, which we enjoyed too as an experience, for we came safely to Tagudin, where the people and the band joined in sending us off, as they had received us, and we were safely taken out through quite a heavy surf and put on board the Coast Guard boat *Negros*, and had a glass with ice in it again.

CHAPTER VIII
INSPECTING WITH THE SECRETARY OF WAR

August thirteenth is a holiday in the Philippine Islands, for it is "Occupation Day," the anniversary of the fall of Manila and its occupation by the American army. The special event is a "camp fire" in the evening at the theater, when the Philippine war veterans gather together and have addresses and refreshments. After a dinner with Tom Anderson at the Army and Navy Club, with its picturesque quarters in an old palace, intramuros, we attended this performance, sitting in the Governor's box and listening to the happy self-laudation of the "veterans," who all wore the blue shirt and khaki of war times.

It was toward midnight when we finally left and went out to our vessel, for we were off for a trip among the southern islands on the cable steamer *Rizal*. We sailed by the light of a full moon, and for a while had a merry bobbery of it outside, after passing Corregidor. Soon, though, we turned a point and had the monsoon following. In the morning we woke to find ourselves steaming past the fine scenery of southern Luzon, with the volcano of Taal in the distance. Several times during the Spanish occupation this volcano dealt death and destruction, and as late as 1911 it claimed many victims.

Our first landing place was at Kotta, on Luzon, where we started ashore in a small launch. It was a beautiful river of palms, but our boat got stuck in the mud and we were delayed. We finally reached the shore and were put into automobiles. Then it was that I began to feel as if I had joined a circus parade. Escorted by bands and soldiers, our motors moved slowly along the streets. Everywhere people lined the way, while the windows of the houses fairly dripped with heads.

We passed many little villages that looked prosperous, and processions of carts, showing that the people were active and busy. The road ran over picturesque bridges, for part of it was an old Spanish trail rejuvenated. At all the villages they had made preparations to receive the Secretary, bands were out, the children stood by the roadside and waved, and the women stood in rows to greet us. The municipal buildings were decorated, the piazzas hung with festoons and lanterns. They all wanted to give us *comida* and let off speeches, but it was impossible to live through such hospitalities, so we only halted at each place a few minutes to shake hands.

The stop for the night was Lucena, the home of Mr. Quezon, Philippine Commissioner to the United States Congress. He traveled with us, and we found him very attractive. The general opinion was that Quezon, Legarda, and Osmeña were "playing to the gallery" for political capital, but at the same time they were supporting our administration. It is a good deal like some of our friends in Congress, who make speeches along lines that they know are absolutely untenable.

After climbing into a bandstand, where we stood surrounded by people peering up at us, flowery speeches began, demanding independence. They were the first of the kind we had heard. The Filipinos are good speakers and keen politicians. Among other remarks, an orator said: "Many things occur to my mind, each of which is important, but among them there is one which constitutes a fundamental question for the Filipinos and the Americans. It is a question that interests equally the people of the United States and the people of the Philippine Islands. It is a question of life or death for our people, and it is a question also of justice, for the people of the United States. The fundamental question is evidently, gentlemen, the question of a political finality of my country....

"We are very grateful for your visit, Mr. Secretary, and we hope that the joy that we felt on your arrival may not be clouded, that it may not be tempered, but rather that it shall be heightened, by seeing in you a true interpretation of the desires of the Philippine people, hoping that on your return to the United States after your visit to the Philippine Islands, you will tell the truth as regards the aspirations of the Philippine people."

In answering, the Secretary talked about the different subjects of interest, such as the agricultural bank, land titles, etc. He continued:

"It is very gratifying to me, coming from America, and representing the Government in the position in which I stand, to hear such testimonials as you have given in regard to the men that America has sent to assist you in advancing your interests.... America has been careful to send men in whom confidence can be reposed according to their previous character; and I want to say to you further, that America has given you here just as good government as she has given to her people at home.[22] In all established governments fair and just criticism is welcome and I shall not therefore bear any spirit that would be resentful of any just criticism.

"I shall be very glad while I am here to meet those who have the real welfare of the Islands at heart and the development of this country. I have many things to do and the time is comparatively short, but I shall endeavour so to conduct affairs as to be able to give audience to all law-abiding people who may desire to make any representations to me. I shall be at convenient periods here where I shall be accessible, and any communications which are addressed to me personally will receive proper consideration. Now that states in a general way the object of my visit and the disposition that I propose to make of my time while here. General Edwards, who is with me, as you know, is the Chief of the Insular Bureau. Certainly he, more than any other man in America, understands conditions in the Philippines, and his whole time, thought and mind are concentrated upon the problems connected with your welfare, and he is working all the time to advance your interests. His familiarity with conditions from the time of America's occupation, the establishment of civil government, the settling of the various commercial questions that have arisen from time to time, make him the most effective champion for the Philippine interests in America, and he has not hesitated in Congress whenever your interests are at stake, to stand up and contend for your interests with vehemence that ought to make him eligible to all option as a Philippine citizen....

"You have there a brilliant representative (Mr. Quezon), who is capable of presenting your views and aspirations, and of enforcing your wishes with the most cogent arguments of which your cause is susceptible....

"Now as to immediate independence: we Americans understand by immediate, right away—to-day. Do you want us to get up and leave you now—to depart from your country? You would find yourselves surrounded by graver problems than have hitherto confronted you, if we should do so. I don't positively assert, but I suggest that you yourselves pause, and think whether you might not be reaching forth and grasping a fruit which, like the dead sea fruit, would turn to ashes upon your lips."[23]

It was at Lucena that my husband and I went to Captain and Mrs. S.'s house for the night. We sat on the piazza by moonlight, among beautiful orchids, listening to the band playing in the distance, and gossiping. I was interested in the servant problem, and Mrs. S. had much to tell me that was new.

"Our native servants would much rather have a pleasant 'thank you' than a tip," she said; "if a tip is offered, the chances are that it will be refused, for the boys feel that they would do wrong to accept it. They are very keen, though, about their *aguinaldos*—presents—at Christmas. Every native who has done a hand's turn for me during the year will turn up Christmas Day to wish me a *feliz Pasquas*, and I am expected to give him a present. My whole day is for my servants and their children, who seem to multiply at that time. When I asked my *cochero*, 'Lucio, how many *niños* have you?' he answered, 'Eleven, señora.' 'But how many under fourteen, Lucio?' 'Eleven, señora!' He wanted all the presents that he could get," she laughed.

"But if they don't take tips, do they get good wages?" I asked.

"Not according to American ideas. A Filipino boy will work for small pay, and stay a long time, in a cheerful home atmosphere. They are good servants, too," she continued, "if you take the trouble to train them. I trained a green boy to be a good cook by taking an American cook book and translating it into Spanish. They have a great reverence for books, and that boy thought he was very scientific. I've had him many years. We loaned him money to build his hut near us. He was a year paying it off, but he paid off every cent. Now he has four children for Christmas gifts. When I went away on a visit, he asked me to bring him a gold watch from America. So many years with us gave him that privilege. As we were gone some time I think he feared we might not return, so he wrote us a letter." Seeing my interest, she got the letter and read it to me:

"My Dear Sir Capt.:

"In accompany the great respect to you would express at the bottom. It is a long time since our separation and I'm hardly to forget you because I have had recognized you as a best master of maine. So I remit best regard to you and Mrs. and how you were getting along both, and if you wish to known my condition, why, I'm well as ever.

"Sir Capt. If you will need me to cook for Mrs. why I'll be with you as soon as I can find some money.

"Please Sir Capt.
"Will you answer this letter for me?
"Very respectfully
"Yours, Pedro."

"On returning from the United States I took Pedro back," Mrs. S. went on, "but I found I needed extra house boys. The first who presented himself was Antonio, aged seventeen. He was a very serious, hard-working boy, whose only other service had been a year on an inter-island merchant ship. I took him at once, for servants from boats are usually well trained. He turned out well, and in a few months asked if he could send for his little brother to be second boy to help him. I said he could, so in due time Crispin smilingly presented himself. No questions passed as to salary or work. He was installed on any terms that suited me. A few weeks later, Antonio asked if he could bring his cousin in just to learn the work, so that he could find a place. I consented, and in time came Sacarius, gentle and self-effacing, and apparently intent on learning, and always handy and useful. Again a favour was asked, this time that the father of Antonio might come as a visitor for a three weeks' stay. He was very old, would not eat in my house, only sleep in the servants' room, so again I consented. Father must have already been on his way, permission taken for granted, for his arrival was almost simultaneous. I found him sitting in my kitchen in very new and very clean white clothes, the saintliest old tao, with no teeth, white hair, and a perpetual smile. He rose and bowed low to me, but he couldn't speak Spanish or English, so called his son to him to salute me for him formally. I returned it and made him welcome to my house. He bade them tell me he had journeyed far to tell me of his gratitude for my goodness to his family and that he had such *confienza* in me that he had instructed his sons never to leave me. The old fellow enjoyed himself thoroughly, and spent so much of his son's money that Antonio shipped him home in a week."

"Are they spoiled by living with Americans?"

"Yes, but it shows most in their clothes. Antonio dresses almost as well as his master," laughed Mrs. S. "But he does not attempt to work in his best clothes, wearing the regulation *muchacho* costume without objection, even though some of the army officers' muchachos are allowed to dress like fashion plates, and clatter round the polished floors in their russet shoes. A muchacho will spend his whole month's pay for a single pair of American russet shoes. They love russet, and the shoe stores flourish in consequence."

"How about their amusements?" I inquired.

"Whenever they can get off they go to baseball games and the movies. The little girls wear American-made store dresses now, and great bunches of ribbon in their hair, white shoes, and silk stockings. Some families who in the early days had hardly a rag on their backs now own motors. I don't believe you could force independence on them! The señoritas trip home from normal school with their high-heeled American pumps, and paint enough on their faces to qualify for Broadway. The poor children have to swelter in knitted socks, knitted hoods, and knitted sweaters, just because they come from America. Filipino children are wonderful, though—they never cry unless they are ill. They are allowed absurd liberty, but they don't seem to get spoiled. The Filipina women love white children intensely; the fair skins seem to charm them, and they really can't resist kissing a blond child."

We certainly enjoyed our stay at Lucena. Mrs. S.'s house was so clean and homelike, with its pretty dining room and its broad veranda, and the big shower bath which felt so refreshing. We went to sleep that night watching the palm leaves waving in the moonlight.

In the early morning we all got into automobiles again and ran over fine roads built since the American occupation. We left the China Sea and crossed the island to the Pacific, climbing a wonderful tropical mountain, where, by the way, we nearly backed off a precipice because our brakes refused to work, and we frightened a horse as we whizzed on to Antimonan. The churches here had towers something like Chinese pagodas, and the big lamps inside were covered with Mexican silver. All these island towns have a presidente and a board of governors, called *consejales*, and each province has a governor.

Manila hemp is one of the principal products of this prosperous province, and it is chiefly used to make rope. The plant from which this hemp is made looks very much like a banana plant. The stalk is stripped and only the tough fibers are used. They employ the cocoanut a good deal to make oil, which is obtained from the dried meat, called copra. They had a procession of their products here at Antimonan, which was very interesting.

The hemp and cigar importations were first carried on by Salem captains in the fifties. The great American shipping firm in those days was Russell, Sturgis, Oliphant and Company. The Philippines were out of the line of travel, however, and few people went there except for trade. In fact, as far as I know, only one book was written by an American about the islands before the American occupation.

On the *Rizal* next morning, when I looked out of my porthole at dawn, it seemed to me as if I were gazing at an exquisite Turner painting. Mount Mayon[24] was standing there majestically, superb in its cloak of silver mist, which changed to fiery red. It is the most beautiful mountain in the world, more perfect in outline than Fuji. Mrs. Dickinson was so inspired by its beauty that she wrote a poem, a stanza of which I give:

"Mount Mayon, in lonely grandeur,
Rises from a sea of flame,
Type of bold, aggressive manhood,
Lifting high a famous name
'Bove the conflict of endeavour
Ranging round its earthly base,
Where heartache and failure ever
Stand hand-clasped face to face."

LANDING AT TOBACO.

Our landing at Tobaco was made in the most novel way. As the water was shallow and the *Rizal* could not get into the dock, three carabaos hitched to a wagon waded out till only their noses could be seen; we stepped on to the two-wheeled cart and sat in state on chairs while we wiggle-waggled through the water to the shore. There we went to the town hall and had a banquet with many brown men and a few little brown women. The governor of the province spoke, and General Bandholtz responded in Spanish for the Secretary, who had gone ahead to close a government coal mine that was not proving successful. After the banquet we had an enchanting automobile ride, through quaint villages at the foot of the great mountain to Albay, where a review of the scouts was held by the Secretary in the setting sun.

When our party dispersed for dinner L. and I were "farmed out" to the superintendent of schools, Mr. Calkins. The houses built for Americans were all of wood with broad piazzas, much like summer cottages at home, with the hall in which we dined in the center and the bedrooms leading off it.

So much has been written about the schools and the wonders in education in the Philippines that I shall not try to enlarge on this interesting theme, other than to add my tribute to the government and the teachers, and also to the people who are wise enough to take advantage of the opportunities offered. Each little Juan and Maria, with their desire to learn, may soon put to shame little John and Mary, if the latter are not careful.

"It has not been a fad with them, as we feared it would be," one of the teachers told me; "they have stuck to it. Many grown-ups in the family make real sacrifices to keep their juniors in school. My little Filipina dressmaker is educating all her sister's children and sending her brother to the law school. At first, too, we feared there would only be a desire to learn English and the higher branches, but with a very little urging they are learning domestic science and the trades, showing that they have a mind for practical matters after all."

I begged her to tell me more about the natives, since she understood the people so well, and what she said is worth repeating.

"Even in his grief the Filipino is a cheerful creature," she began; "curiously enough, too, a death in the family is an occasion for general and prolonged festivities. An orchestra is hired for as many days as the wealth of the family permits, and a banquet is spread continuously at which all are welcome, even former enemies of the deceased. Strangers from the street can come; I've often wondered if the beggars imposed on this custom, but there are very few of them, and they seem to respect it. The music drones on day after day. Sometimes only one instrument will be left, the other players going out to smoke, or eat, or rest; but they reassemble from time to time and keep it going. There is always much dancing, for the natives are great dancers and were not the last to learn the one-step and hesitation. Even in their heel-less slippers they are very graceful. Of course masses are said, for they firmly believe that these will take their departed to heaven. With this belief they are so happy, knowing the dear one is better off in heaven than here, that Chopin's funeral march is quickly turned into waltz time, and the *fiesta* waxes merry!

"In Spanish times each district had its band, which always played at the church festivals. Each church had its patron saint, and there was always a saint's day fiesta going on in some district. In the churchyard booths were spread as at our country fairs. Everything from toys to all kinds of chance games, of which they are so fond, was sold. The band played continuously and the people came in crowds. The Americans have catered to this spirit in the yearly carnival which is given every February. This carnival is more than a fiesta, though, for it is also an exhibition of their produce and handiwork. Their hats have always been famous, as has their needlework, and under American encouragement the basket-work exhibit has become one of the finest in the world. Some hemp baskets, woven in colours, look as if they were made of lustrous silk. I can't say which I like best, the finest of our Alaskan Indian, or Apache, or Filipino baskets. Their shell work is lovely, too, and their buttons are coming into the world's market for the first time.

"The Filipinos are also learning at the School of Arts and Trades to carve their magnificent woods most skilfully, and are making furniture which will soon be coming to the States. In the early days a few Chinamen had the monopoly of furniture carving and making. They copied the very ornate pieces brought to Manila by the Spaniards from Spain and France in the native mahogany called nara, and in a harder and very beautiful wood called *acle*, or in a still harder one known as *camagon*, a native ebony. American women soon began to search the second-hand stores and pawn shops for the originals, and had them polished and restored at Bilibid Prison. The expense, considering, was small. A single-piece-top dining table of solid mahogany is often nearly eight feet in diameter and two or three inches thick."

Another of the teachers told me something of her experiences in the early days, when she went out with her father, who was one of the first American army officers there.

"When we landed we lived in an old Spanish palace," she said, "which of course we proceeded to clean. That was the first thing all Americans did on landing. We took eleven army dump-cart loads from the palace of every kind of dirt conceivable. Then we began washing windows and mirrors and lamps, which I am sure had never been touched with water before. The servants were so amazed that they were of very little use. They were mostly Chinese, and had never seen white women work before. The sight of such energy staggered them. Just when we got things running smoothly, father was called home, and our cleaned house fell to his successor's wife, who wept and said she had never been put in such a dirty place.

"It was after this that my real adventures began. Father McKimmon was opening public schools, and wanted English taught. So he went among the army girls and just begged us to give up a few of our good times and do some of this work. I didn't see how I could teach people when I didn't know their language, but he explained how simple it would be, and we could learn Spanish at the same time.

"It was fun to work with the Spanish nuns. They were so interested in us, and their quaint, old-fashioned methods with the children amused me constantly. Arms were always folded when they rose to recite, and it was always 'Servidor de usted'—at your service—before they could sit down. The nuns soon became pupils of ours, too. When the Spanish prisoners liberated by our men from the Filipinos were brought to Manila they were quartered in our school for a hospital. I never saw such starved wrecks. Many of them—young men—had no teeth left.

"More Americans were arriving on every transport, and a most delightful society was forming of army and navy people, government officials, and naval officers of every nation, in addition to the original Spanish population and the small colonies of many countries. There were parties of all kinds, and as we trained our cooks into our own ways we ventured on dinner parties. I shall never forget the first dinner I went to that was cooked in Spanish style. There was every kind of wine I ever heard of, but no water. I wanted some, but it was not to be had. My host apologized for not having provided any, but no one dared drink the city supply. We sat down to table at nine and rose at twelve, and when the men joined us at one they were all much amazed that I made the move to go home.

"I left Manila to visit my brother in the provinces. Traveling in those days was very different from what it is now. After leaving the Manila-Dagupan Railroad there were no motors to go up the mountain; instead of that, I rode an ancient American horse till I was tired and burning with the sun. Then my brother put me in a bull cart, and I sat on the floor of that till the sun was preferable to the bumping. I arrived at four in the afternoon and was put down in an empty room with my trunk and a packing box. Being a good army girl, that packing box had all the elements of comfort, but first there was cleaning to be done. My brother was the commanding officer in that town, his house being at the corner of the Plaza, and an outpost. So he sent me a police party—that is, ten native prisoners and an American sentry; they were armed with brooms and buckets. I said, 'Sentry, this room is very dirty. The Captain sent these men here to clean it for me.' 'Yes, mam,' said the sentry. 'Well,' I told him, 'I want the ceiling cleaned first, even the corners!' He turned to his gentle prisoners with 'Here, *hombres*, you shinny up that pole and *limpia* those corners!' He didn't know much Spanish, but limpia means clean, and is the one essential word. I soon unpacked my box and turned it into an organdie-draped dressing table, after out of it had come all that made the room livable.

"That night I was sleeping the sleep of the very tired when I was awakened by a blood-curdling shout, a gun was thrown to the floor, and a man's voice yelled for help. I simply froze—I couldn't move hand or foot. The voice was in the outpost guard room, just under my own. Of course, I was sure the whole guard was overpowered and being boloed. I waited for them to come to me as I lay there. Then I heard a man's voice call from an upstairs window, 'What's the matter down there?' and the answer, 'Number Four had a nightmare, sir—thought there was a goat on his bunk.' Just as I was going to sleep again I threw out my hand in my restlessness, and to my horror, clasped it round a cold, shiny boa-constrictor. Every large house has one in the garret to keep down the rats. This time I gave the scream and sprang out of bed. But no snake was to be found, and I decided it must have been the bed post. But what a night that was!"

We reëmbarked at Legaspi and sailed on to the island of Samar, which is in the typhoon belt. Catbalogan is a town which has been visited by very severe typhoons and terrible plagues, but by very few people. It is a small place, far away and forgotten, but the island of Samar is where the massacre of the Ninth Infantry occurred—the massacre at Balangiga by the natives in 1902. There were triumphal arches of bamboo and flowers, and speeches in the town hall, Governor Forbes speaking in both English and Spanish.

Afterward eight small boys and girls dressed in red, white and blue danced for us enchantingly the Charcca and the Jota, clicking their little heels and snapping their little fingers in true Spanish style. Delicious sweetmeats were offered on the veranda, real native dishes, and we drank cocoanut milk and ate cocoanut candy, preserves, nuts and cakes. Two half-Chinese girls who spoke English took very good care of us.

As we left we looked out over the sea to the setting sun and watched a lonely fisherman standing on a rock throwing his net.

Next morning from the *Rizal*, we saw across a stretch of calm water the blue ranges of the mountains of Bohol. Native bancas glided silently about, and a straw-sailed boat drifted idly round the point, where the picturesque gray walls of the oldest Spanish fort in the Philippines stood guard. Its sentinel houses at the corners were all moss grown, and pretty pink flowers were breaking out of the crevices of the rocks.

We landed at Cebu, which is the oldest town in the Islands, and passed down a street lined with ancient houses whose second stories arcaded the sidewalk. They were all in good condition, in spite of their age, for they were built of the wonderful hard woods that last forever. In fact, Cebu has the look of a new and prosperous place, for there have been fires which burnt up many of the ramshackle houses and gave a chance to widen the streets and replace the old structures with permanent looking buildings. The American government has done wonders in deepening the harbour and building a sea wall, behind which concrete warehouses are going up.

There was a scramble to a review near the barracks, then another scramble to a reception at the house of the colonel commanding—a very nice but hot occasion—and then still another scramble to the dedication of a really excellent schoolhouse.

A young priest took us to see the famous idol, the small black infant Christ. We went to the convent of the Dominicans near the church, and passed through its pretty, unkempt court, up a staircase with treads and handrail richly carved in a wood which was hard as iron, and black with age. It was handsome work, such as we had been looking for and hadn't seen before. In the sacristy, too, and the robing room, there were screens and paneling with richly detailed carvings. Passing down the galleries of the convent, where we could see some of the friars at work, we entered the special chapel where this holy image is kept. Several doors were taken off a rather gaudily gilded altar, until at last the little figure was revealed. Its back was toward the room and it had to be carefully turned—a small, brown, wooden doll, all dressed in cloth of gold, and bejeweled like the Bambino of Rome. It is considered a most sacred and wonderful heaven-sent idol.[25]

As we had heard speeches by Filipinos and head hunters, I was curious to know what the Chinese would have to say, and that night there was an opportunity to find out, for we were invited to a dinner given by the Chinese merchants. I quote from the speech made by Mr. Alfonso Zarata Sy Cip, which was specially interesting:

"The Chinese have traded with these Islands since long before Confucius and Mencius," said Mr. Sy Cip; "and for centuries we have been coming here and assimilating with the Filipinos, and to-day we are deeply interested in the welfare of the country. The Chinese have been called a nation of traders, the Jews of the East, but we are more than traders. We are labourers, artisans, farmers, manufacturers, and producers.

"A very large percentage of the growth and development of the commerce and material interests of the Islands is due to the efforts of our countrymen.

"The infusion of Chinese blood has strengthened and improved the Filipino people.

"Chinese labour is recognized all over the world as the best cheap labour in existence. Since American occupation of these Islands you have excluded our labour from entering. Why? Not for the reason that it would tend to lower the standard of living among Filipino labourers, because the standard of living among Chinese labourers in the Philippines is higher than among the Filipino labourers. Hence the introduction of Chinese labourers would tend rather to improve conditions in this regard. You do not exclude him for the reason that he works for lower wages than the labourers of the country, because, on the contrary, the Chinese labourer in the Philippines receives higher wages than the native labourer, hence the introduction of Chinese labourers would tend rather to improve the condition of the native labourers as far as wages are concerned. You do not exclude him for the reason that he will not become assimilated with the natives of the country, because centuries of experience have shown that Filipinos and Chinese do assimilate and readily amalgamate, and the result, as I have already said, is an improvement of the Filipino people. If you are excluding Chinese labourers from the Philippines because of political reasons then I confess such reasons, if they exist, have been carefully guarded as secrets from the public.

"Lack of room is not a reason for excluding Chinese labourers, nor is lack of need for their services. In the great island of Mindanao alone it is doubtful if five per cent of the tillable land is under cultivation, and in other places it is the same. A large part of the rice consumed in these Islands is imported from other countries, yet we have here the finest tropical climate in the world and the most productive soil. Let a sufficient number of Chinese labourers come into the Philippines and we will guarantee that in ten years we will be sending rice to the gates of Pekin and Tokyo."

Toward night we sailed on the *Rizal* from Cebu for the land of the Moros. Out in the Sulu Sea, one felt very near heaven when the sky turned hazy gray in the afterglow, and the distant islands mauve, only their peaks flaming like volcanoes from the hidden sun. Then the big stars came out, like Japanese lanterns, and left a comet-like trail upon the dancing waters.

From their holes below the cabin boys, Ah Sing and Sing Song, would pop out like slim white mice with their long black pigtails, with little cot beds tucked under their arms which they would place in rows upon the deck. Ah Sing would say, "Cheih ko koe" (that will do), and Sing Song would answer, "Hsiao hsin" (be careful). Later, when the moon rose out of the sea and the Southern Cross appeared on the horizon, shadowy forms glided silently up the companionway. But the silence did not last. Some one would call to Sing Song in pidgin English:

"Boy! go catchy whiskey, Tansan; top side, talky man little more fat!" And some one else would say to Ah Sing,

"You fool boy, you catchy me one bath."

Ah Sing seemed to understand. He would wag his head and answer, "You good man, no talky all the time, makey me sick." And he would disappear.

At sight of a tall, genial man, the people in their cots would sing out, "Doctor Heiser's a friend of mine, a friend of mine, a friend of mine," etc. American judges, and Filipino congressmen and generals were of the company. Occasionally a whisper, very often a giggle, sometimes a clinking of glasses, and good night kisses, were heard, and then the sand man closed our eyes.

A MORO *DATO* AND HIS WIFE, WITH A RETINUE OF ATTENDANTS.

CHAPTER IX
THE MOROS

On reaching Mindanao, the land of the Moros, we went ashore at Camp Overton, where we were met by army officers and dougherties drawn by teams of six mules. After a hand-shake at the commanding officer's home, we were furnished with a big escort of cavalry and started climbing up, up, among the hills. Soldiers were hidden in the tall grass all along the way to make sure that nothing would happen to "the great White Sultan with the big Red Flag," as the Moros called the Secretary. Army men could not go out alone, even in those days, for they were attacked by bands and killed, principally to get their weapons, which the Moros were very keen to possess. The *datos*, the head men of the Moro tribes, were allowed to have guns, but none of the other natives. A storm came up, however, not long ago on Lake Lanao, at Camp Keithley, and for fear that his boat would upset, General Wood had a great deal of ammunition thrown overboard, which, it was discovered, was subsequently fished up by the natives.

The Moros are Mohammedan Malays. They came in their boats from islands further south, and in 1380 were converted to Islam by an Arab wise man, Makadum,[26] who made his way to Sulu and Mindanao.

One hears then of Raja Baginda, who came from Sumatra in 1450; his daughter married Abu Bahr, the law giver, who established the Mohammedan Church and, after his father-in-law's death, became sultan and founded a dynasty. In the old days the Moros were all pirates and slave traders. Both Spanish and American authorities have tried to suppress slavery, but it still exists. It is said a woman will bring about forty pesos.

A dato's slaves to-day are well treated, and form part of the family. A slave, moreover, has a chance to rise in the social scale, for Piang, whom we met, was once a slave, but became a powerful chief and a friend of the Americans.

The ruler of all the Moros is the Sultan of Sulu, whom we did not see because he was in Europe at the time we were in the Islands. It is said that a few years ago he would sometimes appear in the market on the back of a slave, with an umbrella held over his head. Here he would stay while the people kissed his hands and feet. He may have changed his customs since his trip.

Dampier, who visited the northern islands of the Philippines, has also left us notes of his stay on Mindanao, which are still true in the main. He says:

"The island of Mindanao is divided into small states, governed by hostile sultans, the governor of Mindanao being the most powerful. The city of Mindanao stood on the banks of the river, about two miles from the sea. It was about a mile in length, and winded with the curve of the river. The houses were built on posts from fourteen to twenty feet high, and in the rainy season looked as if built on a lake, the natives going their different ways in canoes. The houses are of one story, divided into several rooms, and entered by a ladder or stair placed outside. The roofing consists of palm or palmetto leaves.... The floors of the habitations are of wicker-work or bamboo.

"A singular custom, but which facilitated intercourse with the natives and vice versa, was of exchanging names and forming comradeship with a native, whose house was thenceforth considered the home of the stranger."

Alimund Din's name stands out in this meager Moro history beyond all others, for he was the first and only Christian ruler in this land. Even before he became a Christian he was a reformer, and suppressed piracy. He not only coined money but had both an army and a navy, and lived in such splendour as probably has not existed since those days, among the Moros.

Alimund Din ruled about the middle of the eighteenth century, in the time of Philip V of Spain. In return for ammunition to enable the Spanish to keep down piracy, he allowed the Jesuit fathers to enter his country. In time, however, they caused trouble among the Moros, and civil war broke out, as Bautilan, a relative of Alimund Din's, preferred the Mohammedan religion to the new ideas of the Jesuits. Alimund Din and his followers took flight in boats, and in time reached Manila, where they interceded for Spanish protection. The Spaniards showered him with presents, gave him a royal entrance into the city, and finally converted him to Christianity. Later, he was sent back, escorted by Spanish ships, but Bautilan's fleet attacked them. As the Spaniards suspected Alimund Din of becoming a Christian not entirely for Christianity's sake, they threw him into prison. The throne was restored to him in 1763 by the English, who occupied this part of the island for a short time.

A MORO GRAVE.

The Moros are not supposed to eat meat or drink wine, although they have been known to drink whiskey and soda with Americans, as well as eat pork and beans on occasions. There are no mosques in this region or holy dancing-girls (who can do no wrong) but there are Moro priests or *panditas* who go from house to house. They have little education, but some of them have traveled. It is the custom for a relative of the deceased to watch and protect a Moro grave for many months. Such a mourner can sometimes be seen squatting near by under a yellow umbrella. The Moros have as many wives as they can afford, but not more than they can afford, for it is an insult to speak of a man's wife as "begging bread."

The Moros are smaller than the East Indian Mohammedans, but are strong and slight, and have fine features. They appear especially cruel and determined because their teeth are black from *buyo*. In war time, many of the women fought beside the men, and it is supposed to be they who mutilated the Americans found dead on the field after battle. The people whom we met on the road with their ponies loaded with hemp seldom smiled and did not bow, but they looked us straight in the eye, and there was no touch of sulkiness about them.

It is very difficult to distinguish the men from the women, as they dress much alike. But you see few of the latter on the road, for being Mohammedans, most of them are kept at home. They are not veiled like other Moslem women, except when first married.

The costumes of the Moros differ to such a degree—and for no reason that I could discover—that it is difficult to describe them. Many wear tight trousers, which are something like those of the Spaniards—so tight that they are sewn on the men and never come off until worn out—and are often bright red or yellow in colour. On the other hand, some wear very loose, baggy trousers or skirts of different shades. Indeed, they are the most gaily dressed people I have ever seen, and their brown skins set off the vivid yellows and greens and reds and magentas and purples of which their trousers and jackets and turbans and handkerchiefs are made. The jackets have a Chinese appearance. The turbans might be old Aunt Dinah's of the South. The sashes, which are woven in the Moro houses, are of silk, bright green and dark red being the predominant colours. They are knotted on one side, generally a kriss or a bolo being held in the knot, and are tied about the waist so tightly that the men look almost laced, and perhaps that accounts for their womanish appearance.

When the American army first occupied this region they treated the Moros well and found them friendly. Take for instance Zamboanga in the south, an especially interesting region. When the American soldiers entered, the Spanish guard left the garrison, and the Spanish population and the priests followed. The Americans found outside the town gates a large barbed wire bird cage, where the Moros had been compelled to leave their arms before entering the town at night, to avoid an uprising. The government of Zamboanga at this time was reorganized by the American officers. A Filipino presidente was appointed, a dato to head the Moros, and a Captain Chinese, as he was called, to manage his people, who were mostly merchants and pearl fishers.

Mindanao was under a military-civil government that worked wonders, for in a few years many of the Moros were brought under control, and they became loyal Americans, although they had always been bitter enemies of the Filipinos and the Spaniards. They say they have found the Americans brave, and have not been lied to by them, and so they seek our protection. Although the Moro and the head-hunter are so different, they are alike in one respect—if they care for an official and have confidence in him they do not want him changed. It is the man they are willing to obey rather than the government. Of course, there are thousands of them, fierce as ever, back in the mountains, and they are still fanatic and wild. Even among those who are under control, the greatest care has to be exercised, for they have the hatred of the Christian deep in their hearts, and they may run amuck at any moment and kill till they are killed; but this is a part of their faith, they ask no quarter, and nothing stops them but death.

Besides the danger of their attack by religious mania they have a great desire for rifles, as I have said, and they are always "jumping" the constabulary, attacking small parties suddenly from ambush and cutting them down with their knives, or killing sentries; so that constant care has to be used, and the sentinels walk at night in twos, almost back to back, so as to have eyes on all sides. A few weeks before we arrived there had been several cases of "jumping."

An American army officer told me the fights with the Moros generally occurred on the trails among the hills; as the foliage is so thick, it is easy for the natives to conceal themselves on either side, sometimes in ditches, and give the Americans a surprise. For this reason, a drill was found necessary for single file fighting. Every other soldier was taught to respond to the order of one and two. When an attack was made, the "ones" shot to the right, the "twos" to the left. This proved successful. The same officer said the Moros would often use decoys to lead the troops astray. Seeing fresh tracks, they would hasten on in pursuit, and be led away from their supplies, while their enemy would be left behind to attack them in the rear. Walking on the mountain trails was very hard on the soldiers' shoes, and on one of these expeditions their boots gave out, so they were obliged to make soles for their shoes out of boxes and tie them on with leather straps.

Up, up we drove; the clatter of the cavalry could be heard in front and behind, and the dougherty, how it did rattle! It was a pretty sight to see the party traveling through the tropical forests and winding across the green uplands, with their pennons and the Secretary's red flag (which made a great impression on the natives, we heard), and the wagons rumbling along, with a rearguard behind and the scouts in the distance. John, the coloured man, snapped his whip, and the mules trotted along, and the air became cooler, and we drove over a plain where real mountain rice was planted. Occasionally a Moro shack could be seen in the distance.

At an outpost, where we stopped to change mules, we saw a beautiful waterfall, perhaps the loveliest that I had ever seen, called Santa Maria Cristina. From a greater height than Niagara it plunged down into a deep valley of giant trees. It reminded me of a superb waterfall near Seattle.

At last we reached Camp Keithley, on the mountain plain, a forlorn lot of unpainted houses with tin roofs and piazzas, but beautifully situated, like some station in the Himalayas. There was splendid mountain scenery disappearing into the distances, and views of the ocean far away, and, on the other side, the great lake of Lanao, an inland sea more than two thousand feet above the ocean, with imposing ranges about. This lake, which has always been the center of Moro life, is surrounded by native villages, and the military post is important and much liked by the officers quartered there.

The Secretary, my husband and I were billeted on Major Beacom, the commanding officer—Mrs. Dickinson had not felt quite equal to the trip. The Major's house was very attractive, and his little German housekeeper gave us excellent food and made the orderlies fly about for our comfort.

We went almost at once to the market place, which was intensely interesting. The gorgeous colours and gold buttons of the costumes were magnificent. Brass bowls for chow were for sale, and betel-nut boxes inlaid with silver, and round silver ones with instruments attached to clean the ears and nose. There are four compartments in these betel-nut boxes—for lime, tobacco, the betel nut, and a leaf in which to wrap the mixture called buyo.

Here we saw the spear and shield dance. The dancer had a headdress that covered his forehead and ears, making him look quite ridiculous, absolutely as though he were on the comic opera stage. With shield and spear he danced as swiftly and silently as a cat, creeping and springing until your blood ran cold, especially as you knew he had killed many a man.

In the afternoon, after reviewing the troops and inspecting the quarters, we crossed a corner of the lake and landed at a Moro village. It was raining hard and the mud was deep. We waded through a street, followed by the people in their best clothes—one in a black velvet suit, another in a violet velvet jacket. I saw only two women in the streets; they were not veiled nor brilliantly dressed, but had red painted lips and henna on their nails. The Moro constabulary here wore red fezzes and khaki, and the officer in command at the time was of German birth.

A MORO *DATO'S* HOUSE.

After we had passed through a bamboo trail, we came into a little open place with three fine Moro houses about, set up above the ground on great posts made of tree trunks. Unlike Filipino houses, they had façades all carved in a rough and handsome sort of arabesque, painted in bright reds and blues, and with pointed roofs and coloured cloths fluttering out of the open spaces, they made fine effects. The long cracks in the walls served as peepholes, where the snapping black eyes of the many wives of the datos were peering out at us. In front, in the little green space, pennons were planted and there was a huge Chinese-looking sea serpent, or dragon, on wheels, with a body of gaily coloured stuffs, and a rearing movable head. This cavorted about in time to the endless noise of the tom-toms. A crowd of natives stood round in their fanciful raiment.

Into one of these houses we were invited. We mounted the ladder to the one large room in the front, into which the sliding panel shutters admitted the air freely, so that it was cool and shaded. Here sat the wives and the slaves in a corner, playing on a long wooden instrument with brass pans, which they struck, producing high and low sounds, with a little more tune than the Igorots. The big room was bare, except for a long shelf on which was some woven cloth and a fine collection of the native brass work, for this is the center of the brass-workers.

We moved on through the little town of nipa houses to visit old Dato Manilibang, whose house was not as fine as those we had seen before, but where we were admitted into two rooms. From the entrance we streaked muddy feet across the bamboo-slatted floor into his reception room, where a sort of divan occupied one side—on which the Secretary was asked to sit. Behind this cushioned seat were piled the boxes with the chief's possessions, and here he sits in state in the daytime and sleeps at night. The women, who were huddled together on one side of the room, wore bracelets and rings, and one was rather pretty.

At dawn we were up and off again. What a day! We had two hours on a boat crossing a lovely lake, surrounded by mountains, on the shore of which some of the wildest Moros live. Our boat was a big launch, a sort of gunboat, which, strangely enough, the Spaniards had brought up here and sunk in the lake when the war came on, we were told, and which had been resurrected successfully. It was a steep climb up the opposite side of the lake, but most of us scrambled up on horses, till we topped the ridge and came to Camp Vickers, a station with fine air and outlook but rather small and pathetic.

The picturesque Moros had gathered here to greet the Secretary, and their wail of welcome was something strange and weird. A dato would come swinging by, followed in single file by his betel-box carrier, chow bearer and slaves. Some of the chiefs rode scraggly ponies, on high saddles, with their big toes in stirrups of cord almost up under their chins, and with bells on the harness that rattled gaily. And, of course, the tom-toms kept up their endless music.

We had two more hours of horseback riding—we hoped to see a boar hunt, but owing to some misunderstanding, it did not come off. Then, after a stand-up luncheon at Major Brown's, we started down the trail again in a dougherty.

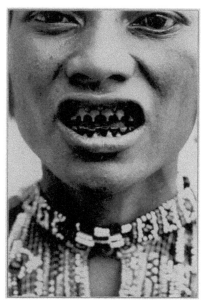

BAGOBO MAN WITH POINTED TEETH.

It was a beautiful drive through this forest on the island of Mindanao. We first crossed open grassy uplands, then dipped down through the great glades of the most tropical forest I have ever seen, with towering hard woods and tree ferns, with bamboos and clinging air plants and orchids, and there was mystery and wonder about the giant growths. The trees seemed taller than the elms of New England or the cedars of Oregon. They dripped with huge-leaved, clinging vines, which grew higgledy-piggledy, covering everything. The grass, too, with waving purple tassels, grew higher than a man's head, twice as high as the pigmy brown people who have their houses in these trees.

The tree-dwellers just referred to are the Manobos and the Bagobos with pointed teeth—for Mindanao is not entirely inhabited by Moros; there are supposed to be no less than twenty-four tribes on this island alone. They build in trees, to escape the spear thrusts of their neighbours through the bamboo floors. We were to make their acquaintance later.

A drenching rain came on that afternoon, through which the escort jogged along, while we clung in our dougherties, nearly shaken to pieces, and reached Malabang, on the other side of the island, as much fatigued as if we had been on horseback all the way. The military post here was most attractive, with the prettiest of nipa houses for the officers, and the parade lined with shading palms, and flower-bordered walks—a charming station. We were quartered with Lieutenant Barry and his wife, a delightful young couple, in their thatched house, and dined with Major Sargent, the commanding officer, who has written some good books on military topics.

The Celebes Sea was calm and lovely when we left Malabang. We passed along the coast of Mindanao toward a long lowland that lay between the high mountains of the island. This was the plain of the Cotobato, a great river which overflows its banks annually like the Nile and has formed a fertile valley that could be turned to good account. The mouth of the river is shallow, so that we were transferred to a stern-wheel boat that was waiting, and began to work our way up, against the rapid current, past low, uninteresting banks that were proving rather monotonous, when suddenly we turned a point and saw the town of Cotobato.

The Moros and the other tribes were in their full splendour here. Soon, down this tropical river, where crocodiles dozed and monkeys chattered and paroquets shrieked, there came a flotilla from the Arabian Nights, manned by galley slaves. On the masts and poles of one of the barges floated banners, and under the canopy of green sat a real Princess. Some of the boats were only dugouts with outriggers, but they were decorated, too, and all the tribes were dressed in silks and velvets of the brightest colours.

There was great excitement and much cheering as we approached the landing stage, and the troops stood at attention, while the rest of the shore was alive with the throng of natives in all the colours of the rainbow. The Secretary inspected the troops, and we saw for the first time the Moro constabulary, wearing turbans and sashes, but with bare legs; nevertheless, they looked very dashing. Indeed, the Moros were so different in character and appearance from any people we had seen before that they might as well have come down from the stars.

The Secretary was taken to meet the datos, as they stood in line beneath the great trees, with the motley crowds of retainers behind them, in such a medley of colours as I had never imagined before. The sunlight filtered through the trees upon the barbaric costumes, while the gaily dressed women stood behind the men and peered over them. The brown men looked dignified and very self-respecting, too, although the scene was like the setting of a comic opera, where the imagination had been allowed to run riot.

There we saw Dato Piang and Gimbungen, a very fat dato—what a delightful bug-a-boo name—also Ynock, whose ear had been cut off in a fight, we were told; but strange as it may seem, he said he had clapped it onto his face again and tied it on, and it had grown there. So it hung attached somewhere down on his cheek, and gave him a very peculiar appearance. When the Moros conquered the Filipinos, this dato had the captured women stripped and made to walk before him, and then took them off to the mountains. When he was taken prisoner later by the Filipinos, he was compelled to work in chains in the streets.

Under a canopy the Princess received us, a native woman whose descent was traced for many hundreds of years—said to be a pure Moro, although she looked rather Chinese—and who was recognized as of the highest social superiority, but had little political power. She herself was draped in varied colours, while her chamberlain wore a brocade coat of crimson and gold cloth. Behind her stood her maids bearing the gold betel-nut boxes and chow trays and umbrellas of her rank.

Our luncheon with the commanding officer, Major Heiberg, and his wife, was eaten in delightful little kiosks of nipa and bamboo, which had been built in a small palm grove. The dancing girls of the Princess, who had long nails protected by silver covers, gave us a performance afterward. Curiously enough, their dance was very Japanese in character. Then some Manobos, picturesque in short, skin-tight trousers and bolero jackets, with bags and boxes beautifully worked in bright beads, danced a graceful, monotonous step. The women have a swaying, snake-like dance with waving arms and jingling of bracelets and "hiplets," if I may be allowed to coin the word.

At last, after so many adventures, we found ourselves again on board the *Rizal.* An enchanting spot on this boat was a projection over the bow, on which one could sit curled up high above the water. On this perch we felt like the red-winged sea gulls that circled far above us. We passed over a sea of polished jade, which at night shone with phosphorescence like gleaming silver.

Next morning, August 23d, we approached Zamboanga. Five American ships, all decorated, came steaming out to meet us and fell in behind in order, making a lovely sight on the bright, smooth seas. As we neared the town, we suddenly saw a large flotilla of native boats, with tom-toms beating and thousands of flags fluttering—such a gay sight! Banners of all shapes, streaming and flapping and waving, and such colours and combinations of colours—stripes of green and purple and orange in designs of lemon and red and magenta, serpentine flags and square ones, hung in all sorts of ways, and brightly coloured canopies under which sat the sultans, and green umbrellas and yellow and—bang! off went their small lantankas, tiny native-made cannon—a most exciting reception!

We landed under triumphal arches and were driven in state carriages through lines of school children, who sang and threw us flowers from old Spanish gardens. The post was really beautiful, for it had much left from old Spanish times, and what had been done over had been done with taste. The green parade had a terraced canal passing through it, and avenues of palm; the officers' quarters, smothered in flowering plants and fronting out over the glittering blue sea, were large and airy and finer than any we had seen before. It is considered one of the best posts in the Philippines, and seemed cool and pleasant.

BAGOBOS WITH MUSICAL INSTRUMENTS.

There was the usual procession—first, the troops of the garrison and the constabulary, then thousands of visiting Moros, Bagobos and Manobos, of every colour of skin and clothes, many of them whooping and leaping, and then a tiresome following of hundreds of Filipinos, who had joined in to make a political demonstration. It is said the Filipinos did not wish the Moros to take part in the procession.

Exciting times followed at the meeting after this parade, where both Filipino and Moro speakers were heard. Said a Filipino, addressing the Secretary:

"You have just visited our province and have just learned its conditions; at such places in it through which you have passed you must have seen quite a number of Moros, but I believe that a separation ... could very well be established, to the end that both people, the Christian Filipino and the Filipino Moro, might have the government that corresponds respectively to each of them, for it is a very regrettable thing that on account of the presence of the latter we Christians should be unable to enjoy the liberties that reason and right would grant us....

"I think it is my duty to advise you that the Moros who filed past the grandstand were brought from remote and distant places with the exclusive purpose of giving greater éclat to your reception. Moreover, it must be borne in mind always, in dealing with the affairs of this province, that the

Moros have no political influence, possess no property, nor help pay the expense of the government."

Then Dato Mandi spoke:

"I am here, El Raja Mura Mandi, representing the Moros. As I look about, I see far more Moros than the Filipino contingent, and if that is so, that is the reason it is called the Moro Province. (Tremendous applause from the Moros.)

"When first the Americans came here, from the very beginning, whatever they asked me to do I did. I was loyal to them ever. Now I have heard a rumour that we Moros are in the hands of the Filipinos....

"If the American Government does not want the Moro Province any more they should give it back to us. It is a Moro province. It belongs to us." (Tremendous applause by the Moros.)

Dato Sacaluran threw down the Moro challenge:

"I am an old man. I do not want any more trouble. But if it should come to that, that we shall be given over to the Filipinos, I still would fight." (Applause.)

But Hadji Nangnui, who spoke of himself as "a Samal," made the clearest statement of the Moro position:

"The Secretary of War must look the matter in the face. We are a different race; we have a different religion; we are Mohammedans. And if we should be given over to the Filipinos, how much more would they treat us badly, than they treated even the Spanish badly who were their own mothers and their own fathers in generations? How did they treat them? Think about it! Think twice! We far prefer to be in the hands of the Americans, who are father and mother to us now, than to be turned over to another people." (Applause.)

In the evening we dined delightfully at the Pershings'. After dinner, the Moros danced in the garden the spear and shield dance, and the Bagobo women gave the scarf dance. The Bagobos still offer human sacrifices. Their caps, if tied in a certain way, show how many men they have killed. Their dress is made of cloth which they weave from carefully selected and dyed fibers of Manila hemp, and it is treated with wax in such a way as to make it very smooth and durable. In the glow of the red light from Chino Charlie's famous lanterns, their picturesque costumes, gleaming with bead work, added much to the brilliancy of the scene. They love music and make some large stringed instruments. They also play the flute from the nose, with one nostril stopped up, like the Hawaiians.

BAGOBO WITH NOSE FLUTE.

The dancing under the palms in the garden, by the rippling seas, where the moonlight flooded down radiantly, was quite like a strange dream.

At this dinner I was told the story given by Dean Worcester by which the Moros explain why they do not eat pork:

"Mahamoud had a grandson and a granddaughter.... As he was king of the world, Christ came to his house to visit him. Mahamoud, jealous of him, told him to prove his power by 'divining' what he had in a certain room, where, in fact, were his grandchildren. Christ replied that he had no wish to prove his power, and would not 'divine.' Mahamoud then vowed that if he did not answer correctly, he should pay for it with his life. Christ responded, 'You have two animals in there, different from anything else in the world.' Mahamoud replied, 'No, you are wrong, and I will now kill you.' Christ said, 'Look first, and see for yourself.' Mahamoud opened the door, and out rushed two hogs, into which Christ had changed his grandchildren."

Some verses recited at General Pershing's dinner showed the feeling of army officers about their life in the Philippines. A stanza runs:

"What is it makes us fret so hard
In this benighted land?
It isn't lack of courage
And it isn't lack of 'sand.'
It isn't fear of Moros
Or Bagobos from the hills—
It's the many great discomforts
And the many, many ills."

It is interesting to read in a recent number of the Manila *Times* that Zamboanga, which seemed so like a picture handed down from Spanish days, has absorbed a good share of American progressiveness and is said to stand in a class by itself among Philippine towns. Waterworks and a hydro-electric plant are under construction, the water for which is to be brought along the mountainside, a part of the way through tunnels. To dig these, "experienced Igorot tunnel makers from Benguet were imported," who are getting along amicably with the Moros.

At Jolo, or Sulu, we were again greeted by a Moro fleet and some diving girls and boys.

This seemed the culmination of the picturesque in our trip. The mountains of the island are not high but rather cone-shaped, and as we approached the town we could see behind it the forested slopes of steep Bud Dajo, where the great fight took place in 1906 and many Moros were killed in the crater top of the volcano, to which they had retreated, and from which they challenged and threatened the American forces. It is an island of fierce, piratical Moros, and even the Americans had not tried to do much there. It was dangerous to go outside the little walled town at all, and all the natives coming in were searched for their weapons, which were taken away at the gates. Only a few months before, a fanatic Moro tried to attack the gate guard, but fortunately was killed before fatally injuring any one.

MORO BOATS.

The walled town is a most artistic little Spanish place, built once upon a time by the exiled Spanish Governor Asturia, who made it a gem of a town, with small balustraded plazas and a hanging-garden sea wall, and a miniature wall with battlements and gates, and streets set out with shading trees. The pretty Officers' Club and quarters overhung the wall. The gates of the town are closed at night, and all the natives must leave for their houses outside before the "retreat," but there is a native market and a town built out on piles over the water, which we visited. We drove out to a plain, palm-fringed and backed by mountains, that overlooked the sea, where there was a review of the cavalry and a large company of mounted Moros, who carried many American flags among their waving banners. Within the walls, in a grandstand in the little plaza, where the natives thronged, there was a meeting between the Secretary and the chief datos; and the Hadji, who had been Vizier of the Sultan, made a wise speech, full of promise of loyalty. Our Governor had won the good will of the people about him and the Hadji said that when his people were certain of our good intentions they would come in willingly and be loyal—but, for so many years, they had been misled by previous rulers.

We amused ourselves by going to Chino Charlie's and buying lanterns, and lunched at the Officers' Club. Afterward we went out on the pier inhabited by the Chinese and looked for pearls—Jolo pearls are famous—but we saw none of real value. We watched the Chinamen drying copra, and went through their market, where water slugs were for sale. Finally, we sailed across the bay. Our visit to the Moros was full of colour to the end, for the sun was setting gorgeously as we put out to sea.

CHAPTER X
JOURNEY'S END

The little coral island of Bancoran lies in the middle of the Sulu Sea, quite outside the usual routes of travel. It is inhabited only by birds, and people seldom or never go there. But we wanted to obtain, if we could, some new species of gulls or terns for the Bureau of Science at Manila, and also to enjoy the mysterious sea gardens which are found among the southern reefs. Just after tiffin the island was sighted, lying quite alone by itself in milky green water. The ship stopped and launches were dropped overboard, and a glass-bottomed boat which had been brought along for our use.

The afternoon was ideal—the sky blue and fleeced with snowy clouds piled high, while the intense sun shining on the water flashed back a hundred shades of blue and green and mauve. On one side of the island, which floated like an emerald among sapphires, outstanding rocks chafed the seas into foaming surf, while on the other a long, narrow beach lay shimmering, pale yellow in the sunlight. The island itself was covered with a thick jungle of trees, which were dotted with thousands of resting birds. As we drew nearer they saw us and were afraid, rising and soaring and circling in the clear, pure air, and crying out at us. Flock after flock of sea fowl flew wonderingly over our small craft, their white breasts tinted green with the light reflected from the water.

It was like a Robinson Crusoe island, lost out there in the lonely sea. But there were shells of huge turtles, and bones of birds, which suggested that sometime a feast must have been held there, so it was not wholly undiscovered and unexplored. Among the great roots of the trees the birds had built their nests from leaves. The eggs in some of them were white and about the size of hens' eggs. Several varieties of boobies and terns were found, some brown with green-blue eyes, others ivory-white. A few specimens were shot, and one or two were taken back alive to the *Rizal* for the museum. Previous to this visit the ornithologists had never known to what islands the boobies and frigate birds came to nest, although the scientists had long been searching for the place, so the expedition was well worth while.

But the sea gardens interested me more than the birds or even the island. If Alice could have had her choice in entering Wonderland, she would surely have selected a doorway leading through a glass-bottomed boat, instead of dropping down a rabbit's hole. Beneath the water, which was crystal clear, we could see a strange country with new flowers and peculiar creatures. Where it was sandy and shallow we saw below us fields of green sea grass, on which the fairies must surely have used lawn-mowers, it was so neatly kept.

Interspersed among the fields were beds of feathery, lace-like vegetation unnamed in the language of our party. Passing one expanse after another of this submarine pasturage, we saw depressions in the coral, where tiny fishes played or unknown water creatures had established a little world for themselves and were living in its narrow confines quite unconscious of what went on in the surrounding vastness.

Drifting on into deeper water, we came to a ghost-like gray world of curls and feathers, trembling with life, a forest of pale trees and swaying brown ones, of high hills and dark valleys, made by coral reefs. Pretty rock gardens came into view, where there were cabbages with blue edges, sea anemones and purple fans, a huge toadstool, a giant fungus, and a cactus plant—at least, that is what they looked like to us. There were rainbow shells, too, half hidden, and great blue starfish clinging to the rocks. In and out among the sponges and the brown coral branches, which were so much like antlers, swam curious fishes. Such gorgeous colours—so vivid and in such brilliant combinations! Some were big green fellows, with needle noses; others were electric blue and silver; there were black and yellow ones, too, and striped fishes that looked like sly prisoners dodging their keepers.[27]

ONE DAY'S CATCH OF FISH.

We passed the greater part of the afternoon marooned on this far-away island, some of us going bathing off the shallow, sandy beaches in the clear water. As evening came on we regretfully left the fairy island of Bancoran, and sailed away by the rising moon.

The Penal Colony on Palawan, which I have described in another chapter, was our next point of interest. We left there behind schedule and met a stronger current than we had expected, sweeping down the coast of Panay, so that it was no wonder that we were late in approaching Iloilo. This was especially unfortunate, for very generous preparations had been made there for the Secretary's reception and an interesting series of events arranged, all of which was upset by the delay.

It was sunset when we finally sighted the town. As we cruised up the steeply palisaded coast, with the low-lying foreground of Panay on the other side, backed by its fine ranges of mountains, the effects were most beautiful. The old Spanish fort on its point looked mysterious in the afterglow, and the skies were magnificently alight. A fleet of much beflagged launches and steamers came out to meet the Secretary, whistling a welcome, and turning, escorted the *Rizal*.

Next to Manila, Iloilo is the most important port in the Islands, and has a better climate than its rival. The people here are supposed to be wealthier and more aristocratic than elsewhere. The Payne bill, which had been in operation only a short time, had brought such a return of prosperity to the land, and especially to the planters of this fertile province, that they were all very enthusiastic about Americans, and did all they could to express their gratitude.

VIEW IN ILOILO, ILOILO, SHOWING HIGH SCHOOL GROUNDS.

We were invited for dinner at half after seven, but it was an hour later before we sat down to the long table in the large and rather empty room, with its handsome Venetian mirrors at either end, and its sliding shutters wide open to the night. There were no ladies present except those of our party. We could never tell how things would be arranged,—sometimes there would be Filipina ladies, and sometimes there would not; sometimes the ladies would all be placed together at one side of the table, and again they would be seated next to the men. While waiting for dinner to be announced, we sat about in an airy room, with half-dressed servants peeping in at us, and a phonograph playing Caruso records.

After dinner we had a long drive out through the town, which seemed quite business-like and prosperous. They had rebuilt some of the fine, large, wide-open houses, most of which had been destroyed by the insurrectos. (On the nearby island of Negros, we were told, there were many fine *haciendas* with great houses full of carved work which I was sorry not to see.) Passing through suburbs of nipa houses standing up on their stilts in the moonlight, we came to a plaza gaily illuminated, and to our destination, a mansion approached by a triumphal arch. In the best houses the living rooms are on the second floor, just as in the poorer ones they are raised above the ground on stilts. So here we went upstairs to a great room hung with festoons of flags, where the little women in their bright and varied dresses passing and repassing made a gay scene. It was here, indeed, that we saw some of the prettiest and best dressed women whom we met on our trip.

Most of the following day was spent cruising along the coast of Panay, passing between its fine outlying islands, which reminded us of the Inland Sea of Japan. In the afternoon we came to the entrance of the river on which Capiz is located. The Secretary crossed overland on the first train to run on the new railway, in order to drive in the silver spikes that completed the line.

No dinners had been planned there for those of us who had come by ship, so we did not start up river until half after eight. Capiz is only four miles from the mouth, but they were the longest miles we had ever experienced, for by some mistake the pilot did not arrive, so we went in a *Rizal* launch without one. We just struggled along as well as we could in the dark till the moon came up, which only mystified us the more with its deceptive shadows. Half a dozen times we ran deep into mud banks, and the sailormen were forced to jump overboard and shove us off. They did not appear to enjoy doing this, and no wonder, for it was a crocodile river.

Swarms of fireflies, which gathered on favourite trees, made a very Christmas-like effect with their throbbing lights. They were lovely, too, in the dark shore shadows, and made sparkling reflections in the black river stream. Watching them we could almost forget our troubles.

Finally, after much winding round and backing off, we turned a bend and saw a line of little twinkling lights strung along the shore and on floating barges, giving quite a Venetian effect and showing us the town by their reflection. Landing, we walked across the grassy square to the provincial building, with its open courtyards, where there was to be a ball. We danced a rigodon as usual, and stopped late with the Governor General, who liked to show his interest in these functions, of which the Filipinos think so much. There were three bands, which vied with each other for applause.

THE OLD AUGUSTINIAN CHURCH, MANILA.

Next morning we got away early on our last leg for Manila and the end of our never-to-be-forgotten journey in the Land of Pine and Palm—that far-away, unfamiliar country where your head gets full of strange thoughts, your body of queer feelings, and your heart has great longings.

We crowded everything we could into those few last days in Manila, for we were loath to think of leaving anything undone. Besides packing and shopping, there were teas and dinners, and the army and navy reception. This was lovely, for it was held in the courtyard filled with trees which were hung with dim lanterns. The good looking officers with their white duck uniforms and brass buttons added to the attractiveness of the scene. The men of our party were even busier than we, for they had several banquets to which we were not invited. In my husband's journal I find the chronicle of a typical day. After describing the events of a busy morning, he says: "In the afternoon, there was a reception to meet the constabulary, at four; the opening of the new hospital, a most complete and wonderful one, at half after four; the laying of the corner stone at five for the new hotel, which is a very ambitious project and will make all the difference in the world as far as touring in the Philippines is concerned; in the evening, a dinner, and after that a reception, and a dance."

Manila seemed more picturesque, and to have even more atmosphere, as I came to know it better. The old walls and churches and plazas and corners and quarters; the Pasig with its cascos and bancas plying about; the narrow streets winding through the suburbs, with old moss-covered walls, and peeps of tangled gardens within, and balustraded terraces, and the bowers of the pink blossoming "chain of love." It is indeed well-named the Pearl of the Orient.

BIBLIOGRAPHY

ATKINSON, F. W.: The Philippine Islands

ALEXANDER, MARY C.: The Story of Hawaii

ALEXANDER, W. D.: Brief History of the Hawaiian People

AMERICAN GIRL, AN: Seven Weeks in Hawaii

BANCROFT, HUBERT H.: The New Pacific

BRIGGS, CHARLES W.: Progressive Philippines

BLAIR, EMMA H.: The Philippine Islands

BARRON, DAVID: History of the Philippines

BISHOP, ISABELLA L.: The Hawaiian Archipelago

BLACKMAN, WILLIAM F.: The Making of Hawaii

COAN, TITUS: Life in Hawaii

COAN, T. M.: Climate of Hawaii

—— Hawaiian Ethnography

CASTLE, WILLIAM R., JR.: Hawaii Past and Present

CHAMBERS, H. E.: Constitutional History of Hawaii

CROW, CARL: America and the Philippines

CHAMBERLIN, FREDERICK: The Philippine Problem

DAUNCEY, MRS. CAMPBELL: The Philippines

DEVENS, JOHN B.: An Observer in the Philippines

DAY, MRS. E. F.: Princess of Manoa

EMERSON, N. B.: Unwritten Literature of Hawaii

FEE, MARY H.: A Woman's Impressions of the Philippines

FOREMAN, J.: The Philippine Islands

FORNANDER, ABRAHAM: The Polynesian Race

HAWAIIAN ANNUAL for 1915

HAWAIIAN ISLANDS, Report of Commission of Agriculture and Forestry

HAWAII, a Primer—answers to queries

HITCHCOCK, C. H.: Hawaii and its Volcanoes

JERNEGAN, PRESCOTT F.: A Short History of the Philippines

JORDAN AND EDERMANN: Aquatic Resources of Hawaii

LIBRARY OF CONGRESS: List of books on Hawaii

LINDSEY, FORBES: The Philippines

LE ROY, JAMES A.: Philippine Life in Town and Country

—— Americans in the Philippines

LAWRENCE, MARY S.: Old Time Hawaiians and their Wok

LYMAN, H. M.: Hawaiian Yesterdays

MOSES, MRS. M. E. B.: Unofficial Letters of an Official's Wife

MAUS, L. M.: An Army Officer on Leave in Japan

MUSICK, JOHN R.: Hawaii: our New Possession

MATHER, HELEN: One Summer in Hawaii

ROBINSON, ALBERT G.: The War and the People

STODDARD, C. W.: South-sea Idyls

SAWYER, FREDERICK H.: The Inhabitants of the Philippines

STEVENS, J. E.: Yesterdays in the Philippines

TAFT, MRS. WILLIAM H.: Recollections of Full Years

WESTERVELT, W. E.: Legends of Old Honolulu

WORCESTER, DEAN C.: The Philippines, Past and Present

WILLIAMS, D. R.: The Odyssey of the Philippine Commission

YOUNG, LUCIEN: The Real Hawaii

FOOTNOTES:

[1] When the mamo became rare the natives began to substitute the light yellow feathers growing under the wings of the *o-o*. This bird is now extinct.

[2] In the first Reciprocity Treaty with Hawaii, which was signed in Grant's administration, there was no reference to Pearl Harbour. It was when the treaty was renewed in a revised form during the administration of President Harrison, that Hawaii ceded Pearl Harbour to the United States as a naval base.

[3] General M. M. Macomb was in command from 1911 to 1913, General Frederick Funston during 1914, General W. H. Carter followed and General J. P. Wisser is there in command to-day.

[4] Even to a late date this custom has been known in civilized countries. In France a figure of one's enemy was modeled in wax and was slowly melted before the fire while being "prayed to death."

[5] The legend which ascribes the creation of man to Kane is only one of many Hawaiian creation myths, in which other gods figure as fathers of the human race.

[6] A. Fornander, "The Polynesian Race."

[7] Guam belonged to Spain until Colonel Thomas Anderson stopped there on his way to the Philippines with the first United States troops. The Spanish governor had not even heard that war was declared, and when the ships fired, he thought it was a salute in his honour. He surrendered the fifteen small islands; fourteen were given back to Spain in the Treaty of Paris and they were sold to Germany. Guam has an excellent harbour. It is under the control of the United States Navy at present. Marines are stationed there.

[8] The party at present in power in the United States appears to have given very little attention to the Islands, except as a source of income for deserving Democrats, if we may judge from the latest Democratic platform. That document contains the promise, "as soon as practicable, to

give a territorial form of government to Hawaii." For eighteen years they have had it!

[9] When Mr. Dole's term as United States judge expired a few months ago, President Wilson refused to reappoint him, though all Hawaii petitioned for him. The position was given to a Democrat.

[10] Castle says Halemaumau really means, "home of the *Maumau* fern," this fern having a leaf much like the curled and twisted lava in shape.

[11] A trip to the Lake of Bay should be taken and to the fertile valley of the Cagayan. The gorge of Pagsanjan is very beautiful. Los Banos is an old bathing establishment not far from Kalamba, where Rizal was born. It is part of a day's trip from Manila to this hot mineral spring, which was a fashionable resort in days gone by. Now an American military hospital has been built there.

[12] The American coloured troops in the Philippines certainly deserve mention. They were among the best fighters we sent out there.

[13] Koxinga was really one of the most noted characters of the Orient at that time. He was the son of a Japanese mother and a Chinese father, and seldom has China had a man to compare with him in courage, enterprise and ability. At the age of twenty-two, he held one of the highest military commands in his country. With his courage and natural ability it was his purpose to carve out a kingdom for himself. Being as shrewd as he was bold, Koxinga made the acquaintance of a Dominican friar in Amoy, whom he converted into an ambassador and sent to Manila. Fortunately for the Spaniards, Koxinga's career was cut short by his early death, in 1662, while still under forty years of age, and just as he was making preparations to invade the Philippines.

[14] To-day Aguinaldo seems to be a thoroughly "reconstructed rebel," as this incident told by General Anderson's daughter shows:

"While spending the day with friends who have a sugar estate near Kalamba, our party was augmented by Aguinaldo, Pablo Ocampo and another ilustrado whose name I've forgotten. They had come over from Cavite, where Aguinaldo has his farm, to see this estate with its modern sugar machinery. After going over the farm very thoroughly with the party I found myself next the former General at lunch. Conversation was difficult, as he spoke no English and not very fluent Spanish. I timidly asked him in desperation of something to say, if he remembered my father. On learning that he was the first Americano General to fight him, over fifteen years before, he became most interested, and asked very warmly to be remembered. When I told him my father was also retired and settled on his little farm he was pleased and said it was the real life. I think he is sincerely a farmer and will not be lured back to the hazards of political life. He is a modest, quiet, diffident little native of the pure Filipino type. He assured me that his children were making good progress in English and were at school working hard."

[15] After Mr. Taft had made his journey to Rome to arrange the friar land question, he received a remarkable ovation upon his return to the Philippines. When he was appointed Secretary of War, Manila was flooded with posters bearing the words, in various languages, "We want Taft," and such a host of petitions from influential citizens was sent to Washington that Mr. Roosevelt canceled the appointment. It was not until some time later that it was renewed and Mr. Taft left the Philippines to take his seat in the Cabinet at Washington.

[16] It is difficult to realize the importance of the mestizo class in the Philippines. There are about seventy-five thousand Spanish mestizos and half a million Chinese mestizos.

[17] Any one who is inclined to regret American rule in the Islands is cordially invited to read chapter sixteen in Dean Worcester's book, "The Philippines, Past and Present."

[18] The cause of the pneumonic plague is so little known that it may be interesting to mention it here. The disease, it is said, is carried by marmots. It had not broken out since the fourteenth century, because Manchu hunters had for generations been taught not to kill marmots for this very reason. But in late years, with the great demand for furs, new hunters who knew nothing of this, killed the diseased marmots and so caused an epidemic.

[19] The name "Bashee," originally applied to the Batan Islands, was derived from an intoxicating drink of that name made from sugar-cane and berries. It is still used very liberally, especially on all festal occasions. When Dampier's ships first touched these shores the *Bashee* was highly regarded by these ancient mariners.

[20] Although we think of Japanese territory as far away from ours, here it approaches within sixty miles, as I have said, and within twenty-four miles of Guam the Japanese have lately occupied the former German islands of the Mariana group. In Bering Straits we are within three miles of Russian territory. There are two islands, the Diomedes, in the center of the strait, one of which is owned by Russia and the other by the United States. We usually consider both Japan and Russia very far off, but their possessions are in fact almost as near ours as Canada and Mexico.

[21] An interesting passage from Worcester describes this Kalinga dance with more detail:

"Into the ring steps the hero of the occasion, dressed in his best clothes, decked with his gaudiest ornaments, and bearing the shield, lance and head-ax used in the recent fights. Behind him there creeps along the ground a strange, shrinking figure, clad in soiled garments, with a dirty cotton blanket pulled over its head. The hero attracts attention to himself by emitting a squall which resembles nothing so much as the yell of a puppy when its tail is heavily trodden upon. He then begins to speak in a monotonous and highly artificial voice, the tone and cadences of which are strongly suggestive of those of a Japanese actor. With word and gesture he describes his recent exploit, using the shrinking figure beside him as a dummy to represent his fallen foe. When he stops for breath the ganzas strike up again, and when their clangour ceases he resumes his narrative. After concluding his pantomimic discussion of his latest exploit, he describes and boasts of previous achievements. Incidentally he indulges in high stepping and high jumping and displays deadly skill in the manipulation of his weapons. The crowd grows even more excited and, during the intervals while the ganzas are playing, shrieks its approval and shrills its monotonous war cry. Finally when his voice has grown hoarse and his muscles are tired, the principal actor retires and another takes his place. As darkness comes on, a blazing fire is lighted within the cañao circle.

"Ultimately the young and vigorous warriors who participated in the recent fight are succeeded by the old men, who have been kept at home by the burden of years and infirmities. Strong drink has caused the dying fire in their veins to flare up for the moment. Each of them has a history of warlike deeds, which he proceeds to recount. The crowd already knows his story by heart, and when the forgetfulness of age or that of intoxication causes him to falter, prompts him and shouts with laughter at the joke.

"Gradually the *basi* begins to exert its stupefying effect; but so long as the music and dancing, and the shouting continue every one manages to keep awake. At last, food is passed, and in the interval during which it is being consumed the liquor gets a fair chance to work. As the east begins to glow with the coming dawn, men and women fall asleep in their places, or hasten to their homes, and the cañao ends, for the time being at least."

[22] It is not so well known in this country as in the Far East that the fine code of laws which we have given the Philippines was drafted by our great statesman, Elihu Root, with the aid of some suggestions from Mr. Worcester.

[23] I have taken a few remarks from several speeches.

[24] The ascent of Mt. Mayon is dangerous except for experienced mountain climbers. The vista from the summit is said to surpass even the famous view from Mt. Ætna.

[25] The Santo Niño of Cebu has a famous rival in the village of Antipolo where "Our Lady of Peace and Prosperous Voyages" is found. This image was brought to the Islands in 1626 by the Spanish government. It is said the Virgin has crossed the Pacific eight times to and from Mexico and each time "calmed a tempest."

[26] This great missionary is buried on the island of Sibutu.

[27] Worcester writes in regard to fishing: "There are barracudas of seven different species, some of which attain a length of six feet and weigh a hundred pounds or more. Bonitos of four different species have been taken, and afford fine sport. Croakers and groupers (locally known as *lapu-lapu*) are found in great variety. Hardtails and leather-jacks, commonly called *dorados*, are also very abundant. They take the spoon freely and fight well. There are also several species of mackerel and *pampano*, which are excellent table fish; and snappers, of which we have thirty-four known species. The large red snappers fight well. Sea-bass of two distinct species are common. Specimens weighing fifty to seventy-five pounds are frequently seen in the markets. The largest specimen as yet recorded from the Islands weighed three hundred thirty-four and a fourth pounds.

"Swordfish, nine feet or more in length, may be taken during the cooler months. Tarpons up to five feet in length may be taken at the proper season, off the mouths of large streams. The species are distinct from that found in Atlantic waters, and the young take the fly freely.

"The great, or leaping, tunas are met with in large schools during the winter months. The natives call them *cachareta*."